I0796852

PRAYING FOR WISDOM EVERY DAY

WISDOM is far more valuable than silver, and her revenue is greater than that of gold. —Prov 3:14

PRAYING FOR WISDOM EVERY DAY

MINUTE MEDITATIONS FOR EVERY DAY CONTAINING A SCRIPTURE READING, A REFLECTION, AND A PRAYER

•

By

REV. JUDE WINKLER, OFM Conv.

CATHOLIC BOOK PUBLISHING CORP.
New Jersey

CONTENTS

IMPRIMI POTEST: Very Rev. Michael Heine, OFM Conv.
Minister Provincial of
Our Lady of the Angels Province

NIHIL OBSTAT: Rev. Pawel Tomczyk, Ph.D.
Censor Librorum

IMPRIMATUR: ✠ Kevin J. Sweeney
Bishop of Paterson

March 18, 2024

The Nihil Obstat and Imprimatur are official declarations that a book or a pamphlet is free of doctrinal or moral error. No implication is contained therein that those who have granted the Nihil Obstat and Imprimatur agree with the contents, opinions or statements expressed.

(T-141)

ISBN 978-1-958237-64-9

Printed in China 24 HA 1

catholicbookpublishing.com

INTRODUCTION

In Israel there were two major forms of revelation. The first was when God directly revealed His Will in words and actions. This would include the messages that God gave Israel through the prophets. The second form of revelation was discerned through the world around us.

This second form of revelation was wisdom. In its earliest form, it was a collection of sayings learned from life, not unlike the sayings of Benjamin Franklin. As time went on, wisdom came to be understood as an attribute of God which told us who God is and what God wants of us.

This meditation book contains a series of Wisdom sayings on how to live a good and holy life. They tend to be very practical, so that even though they were written over two thousand years ago, they can still be applied to our lives today.

The sayings come from the Book of Proverbs, a collection of Wisdom sayings attributed to King Solomon. These proverbs were probably accumulated over a long period of time, and the oldest might date to around the time of Solomon.

There are sayings from Ecclesiastes, also known as Qoheleth. These sayings were collected much later, and they speak of the difficulties and frustrations of trying to live a good life. They reject the idea that if someone were to live a good life, that person would automatically prosper.

The third source for these sayings is Ecclesiasticus, also known as Sirach or Wisdom of Ben Sira. These sayings were collected during the Greek era, sometime around 200 B.C. The author wanted to show that Jewish wisdom was just as good as Greek wisdom.

May the sayings be meaningful to you and help you along your path to the Lord as you pray them each day.

Fr. Jude Winkler, OFM Conv.

Dedicated to Rev. Melvin Blanchette, P.S.S., who has served as a wisdom figure for many over the years.

VERY word of God has proven to be true. —Prov 30:5a

JAN. 1

REFLECTION. As we begin this New Year and reflect upon how the Word of God became incarnate in the womb of the Blessed Virgin Mary, the Mother of God, it is good to remember how faithful God always has been and will be.

God's Word has always proved Itself to be faithful and true.

PRAYER. *Lord, I dedicate this New Year to Your praise and glory.*

RUDENCE will protect you, and understanding will watch over you. —Prov 2:11

JAN. 2

REFLECTION. Prudence allows us to weigh all the possibilities that we have before us and to choose that which most closely follows the path of the Lord.

Understanding gives us the practical ability to put our plan into action and to evaluate its success as we travel along on our faith journey.

PRAYER. *Protect and guide me, Lord, so that I might always be faithful to Your call.*

HE name of the Lord is a tower of strength; the upright person runs to it and finds refuge. —Prov 18:10

JAN. 3

REFLECTION. The name Jesus is a form of the name Joshua. It literally means that Yahweh saves.

Jesus carried His mission and His message in His name. It is a proclamation of what God has always wanted for us: to be saved from our sin and to live in His love forever.

PRAYER. *Jesus, Son of the Living God, have mercy on me.*

HARM is deceptive and beauty is fleeting, but the woman who fears the Lord is to be praised. —Prov 31:30

JAN. 4

REFLECTION. There are very few proverbs that speak of women in their own right. This is one of those few.

Like the proverbs addressed to men, it speaks of the passing nature of those things that we often hold onto as symbols of our personal value and of the need to make God the center of our lives.

PRAYER. *May I follow the example of holy women such as St. Elizabeth Ann Seton.*

ITHOUT letting them slip out of your sight, safeguard sound wisdom and prudence. —Prov 3:21

JAN. 5

REFLECTION. We all have many things to do. St. John Neuman, whose feast we celebrate today, was incredibly active in the preaching of the Gospel in the eastern United States.

Yet, he never allowed this activity to keep him from his prayer and meditation. Life is too busy not to base it upon a solid spiritual foundation.

PRAYER. *May I always find time to place You first, Lord.*

HEN you are ill, do not delay, but pray to God and he will heal you. —Sir 38:9

JAN. 6

REFLECTION. God does not always say "yes" to what we ask for when we pray.

God will always give us the most loving answer possible. If that is that we will be healed, then we will be healed. If the answer is that we will meet God on the cross of our sickbed, that will be the answer.

PRAYER. *Lord, answer my prayer with Your loving care.*

S WATER extinguishes a blazing fire, so almsgiving atones for sins. —Sir 3:30

JAN. 7

REFLECTION. Sin is an act of hate— hatred of others and even hatred of ourselves (for we are effectively saying that we are nothing but trash and we might as well act like trash).

Giving alms brings us out of ourselves. It reminds us that God created us to be loving and compassionate and not selfish and arrogant.

PRAYER. *Lord, may I never ignore the cry of the poor.*

F YOU reprove an insolent man, he will hate you; if you reprove a wise man, he will love you. —Prov 9:8

JAN. 8

REFLECTION. We can often measure how much our ideas are reflections of our arrogance or of our wisdom.

If we respond to criticism or correction with defensiveness and possibly aggression, then we are being arrogant. If we are willing to examine our ideas with the help of others, then they are based upon wisdom.

PRAYER. *Grant me wisdom, Lord, and uproot arrogance from my heart.*

BETTER is one handful with peace of mind than two handfuls with toil and a chase after the wind. —Eccl 4:6

JAN. 9

REFLECTION. It is important to learn how to be satisfied with what is enough for us. When we seek after and toil for more and more, we often find ourselves frustrated and dissatisfied.

When we remind ourselves to enjoy the simple pleasures of life, we will realize how truly blessed we are.

PRAYER. *Lord, grant me what I truly need and not necessarily what I want.*

ONE who gossips reveals secrets, but a trustworthy person keeps things hidden. —Prov 11:13

JAN. 10

REFLECTION. We know that we are gossiping by applying a simple rule of thumb: is it kind, is it true, is it helpful.

People often use gossip to put another down and feel better about themselves, but it is terribly destructive, both for the reputation of the person being talked about and for the person engaged in the gossip.

PRAYER. *Lord, teach me to be cautious with what I say and why I say it.*

O NOT flaunt your wisdom in doing your work, and do not put on airs when you are in need. —Sir 10:26

JAN. 11

REFLECTION. We are called to be people of humility and integrity.

Humility recognizes that the credit for our successes rightly belongs to God Who gave us the talent and ability to do what we are doing. Integrity helps us present ourselves to others as we really are and not as we wish they would see us.

PRAYER. *May I always be humble and transparent in the way I present myself to the world.*

HE poor man is disliked even by his neighbor, but one who is wealthy never lacks for friends. —Prov 14:20

JAN. 12

REFLECTION. We often judge others by what we can obtain from them. Christ, on the other hand, reached out to the poor for they needed His love and attention the most.

If we wish to be Christ-like, we must make a choice to open our hearts (and at times our wallets) to those who cannot repay us in any way.

PRAYER. *Lord Jesus, let me see You in the faces of the poor and broken.*

LESSED is the one who meditates on Wisdom and reasons with intelligence.

—Sir 14:20

JAN. 13

REFLECTION. We are told in the great commandment that we should love the Lord with our whole heart. The ancients believed that the heart was where one thought and made decisions.

This means that we should love God with our intellect. We should study and reflect upon the meaning of our faith.

PRAYER. *May I love You, Lord, with my heart, my soul, and my strength.*

OR lack of leadership a nation collapses; safety is assured with a multitude of advisers.

—Prov 11:14

JAN. 14

REFLECTION. It is a fundamental error to think that any of us has all the answers. We approach decisions from our point of view, and that is based upon our own way of seeing things.

By seeking advice from others, we show our respect for the fact that the Holy Spirit is working through others as well.

PRAYER. *Holy Spirit, guide me and those around me in our decisions.*

NYONE who strays from the way of prudence will rest in the company of the shades. —Prov 21:16

JAN. 15

REFLECTION. There are consequences for the choices that we make. If we are too rash or too cautious, then we will not be able to find the right path for our actions.

We have to discern our decisions prudently and find the middle path, avoiding the extremes which could lead to ruin.

PRAYER. *Lord, guide my decisions so that they might be prudent and wise.*

O NOT kindle the coals of a sinner, lest you be burned in his flaming fire. —Sir 8:10

JAN. 16

REFLECTION. Our goal in life is to walk closer with our Lord and to help those around us. This means giving a good example and inviting sinners to change their ways.

If we go along with the plans of sinners by encouraging their sinful ways or ignoring their downward spiral, then we will eventually get burned by their choices.

PRAYER. *May I always remember that those around me are my sisters and brothers.*

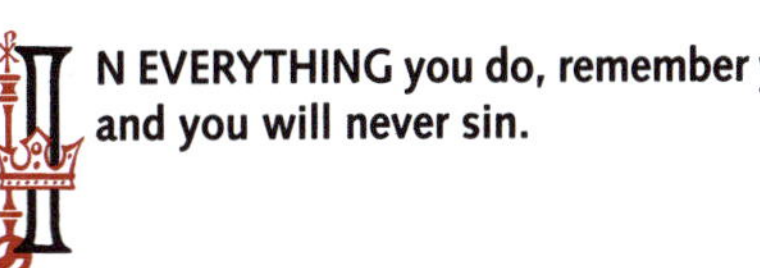

N EVERYTHING you do, remember your end, and you will never sin. —Sir 7:36

JAN. 17

REFLECTION. There was an evangelist in the city of Sydney, Australia who would write the word “eternity” on the walls of the city in chalk to remind people of their ultimate destiny.

If we keep our true goal in mind, then all the choices that we make each day will be made in light of our eternal calling.

PRAYER. *May each day bring me closer to my true eternal destiny.*

VEN at times of laughter the heart may be sad, and joy may end in grief. —Prov 14:13

JAN. 18

REFLECTION. Times of joy and celebration do not last forever. Sooner or later, we will have to face difficulties and grief.

If we are walking with the Lord, then when we laugh or cry, we will be doing it in the Lord. When we laugh, we will be grateful, and when we cry, we will reach out for His consolation.

PRAYER. *Whatever I feel or think or do, may it be in You.*

O NOT babble on in the assembly of the elders, and in your prayers do not repeat yourself. —Sir 7:14

JAN. 19

REFLECTION. It seems as if some people love the sound of their own voices. They never say in ten words what they could say in twenty.

St. Francis taught that Jesus spoke only briefly while He was on the earth. This means that we should weigh our words carefully and be careful not to overdo it.

PRAYER. *May I say few words, Lord, but may those words be filled with wisdom and love.*

O NOT become easily angered, for anger lodges in the heart of fools. —Eccl 7:9

JAN. 20

REFLECTION. If we find ourselves always getting angry at everyday events, then it is probably time for us to seek a bit of help (for our benefit and that of those around us).

We could read a book on the topic, pray for a healing of our anger and resentment, or seek some form of counseling or spiritual accompaniment.

PRAYER. *Lord, bring me Your peace; may my spirit be filled with Your consolation.*

DO NOT fear death's sentence; remember it embraces those who preceded you and those who will come after. —Sir 41:3

JAN. 21

REFLECTION. The martyrs, such as St. Agnes, did not fear death. Rather, they saw it as an opportunity to show witness to their faith.

As we feel the effects of diminishment due to illness or frailty, we have to make choices on how we would like to die and how even our death might give a good example to others.

PRAYER. *St. Agnes, please accompany me through my trials and guide me in my surrender to God's Will.*

RESCUE those who are being led away to death, and save those who are on their way to execution. —Prov 24:11

JAN. 22

REFLECTION. Today is the day of prayer for the respect of the rights of the unborn. We remind ourselves that we are responsible for the protection of the weakest in our society.

There is a Jewish saying that one who saves the life of a single person has saved all of humanity. Every person is precious in the eyes of the Lord.

PRAYER. *Lord, protect those who cannot protect themselves.*

O NOT grow tired of praying, or neglect to give alms. —Sir 7:10

JAN. 23

REFLECTION. In the great commandment we hear that we must love and serve God and love and serve our sisters and brothers.

Only praying while ignoring those around us is a pious form of hypocrisy, but without a spiritual foundation trying to serve others is bound to end in disillusionment and frustration.

PRAYER. *Lord, may I love and serve You and those around me.*

PERSON may plan his own course, but the Lord makes his steps secure. —Prov 16:9

JAN. 24

REFLECTION. St. Francis de Sales taught that each of us must find God in the particular state of life in which we find ourselves. What is good for one is not necessarily good for another.

But no matter which form of life we follow, what we do and who we are must be based upon our relationship with the Lord.

PRAYER. *I consecrate my life to You, O Lord. Please accompany me in all that I do.*

EED advice and accept instruction so that your wisdom may increase in the future. —Prov 19:20

JAN. 25

REFLECTION. St. Paul thought he knew exactly what God wanted of him. Then Jesus appeared to him on the road to Damascus and changed his life entirely.

We have to be willing to listen to the message and advice of others for we never know if they were sent to us as messengers of the Most High.

PRAYER. *St. Paul, guide me in my conversion.*

HE governance of the earth is in the hand of God; he will raise up the right leader over it at the proper time. —Sir 10:4

JAN. 26

REFLECTION. The letters to Saints Timothy and Titus date to the period right after that of the apostles when the Church had to think about the establishment of a hierarchy.

Those who lead the Church are called by God to a ministry of service and compassion. Preoccupations with power and prestige should never cloud their reasoning.

PRAYER. *Saints Timothy and Titus, pray for those who lead the Church today.*

AY your soul rejoice in the mercy of the Lord, and may you never be ashamed to praise him. —Sir 51:29

JAN. 27

REFLECTION. When we experience the mercy of God, we realize that God is giving us something that we do not truly deserve. We don't earn God's forgiveness; it is a gift from a loving God.

There is only one possible way to respond to God's generosity: to be filled with gratitude and praise.

PRAYER. *God, I will praise You and Your compassion forever and ever.*

F YOU search Wisdom out and follow her trail, she will make herself known, and once you have found her, do not let her go.

—Sir 6:27

JAN. 28

REFLECTION. St. Thomas Aquinas was a remarkably brilliant theologian. He wrote an incredible number of books on the truths of the faith.

Yet, he recognized that everything that he had taught and written fell short of the mystery of God's love. Possibly his greatest wisdom was found in his humility.

PRAYER. *St. Thomas Aquinas, guide us to wisdom and humility.*

HE idler will dip his hands into the dish, but he will not so much as lift it to his mouth. —Prov 19:24

JAN. 29

REFLECTION. There are people who act as if the world owes them something, and they will not take the necessary steps to make their situation better.

God has given all of us talents and opportunities, and God expects us to use them well. We are responsible for making this world a better place.

PRAYER. *Lord, give me the will and the energy to do what needs to be done.*

O NOT quarrel with someone without cause when that person has done you no harm. —Prov 3:30

JAN. 30

REFLECTION. There are times when we are angry or anxious and we begin a quarrel with another not because that person deserves it, but just because that person is available at the time.

We must find healthier ways to express our anger because we should not dump it upon someone who is innocent.

PRAYER. *May I always treat people fairly, even when I am having a bad day.*

HE proverbs of Solomon . . .so that the young may gain knowledge and discretion. —Prov 1:1, 4

JAN. 31

REFLECTION. The Book of Proverbs speaks of the need to instruct the young. This was a task which St. John Bosco always took to heart.

We should ask ourselves what we can do to help them learn the ways of the Lord. At the very least, we could include them in our prayers every time we pass a school building.

PRAYER. *St. John Bosco, show us how we might serve the simple and the young.*

VOID reproaching a repentant sinner; remember that we are all guilty. —Sir 8:5

FEB. 1

REFLECTION. Jesus told us to remove the plank of wood from our own eyes before we attempt to remove the sliver from the eyes of another.

Rather than using the flaws of another as an opportunity to judge that person, we could ask ourselves how our own conversion might invite that person to follow our example.

PRAYER. *God, teach me to recognize myself as a sinner in need of conversion.*

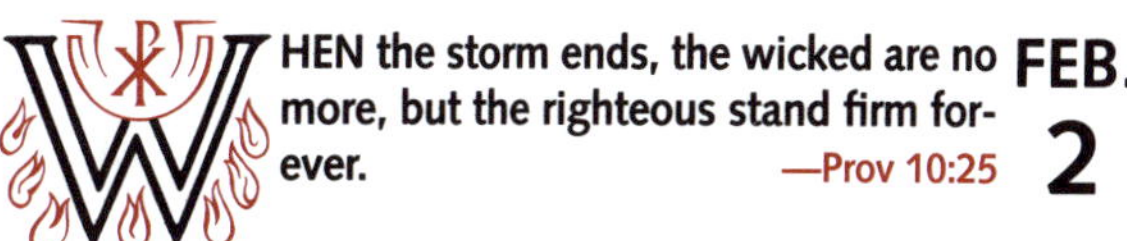

WHEN the storm ends, the wicked are no more, but the righteous stand firm forever. —Prov 10:25

FEB. 2

REFLECTION. Simeon prophesied that a sword would pierce the heart of the Blessed Virgin Mary. She would share in the sufferings of her only Son. But rather than embittering Mary, this wound enabled her to share in our sufferings as well.

We can turn to Mary in our difficulties and know that she will understand and console us.

PRAYER. *Blessed Mother, please accompany us whenever we carry our crosses.*

FALSE scales are an abomination to the Lord, but a true weight is pleasing to him. —Prov 11:1

FEB. 3

REFLECTION. The Book of Proverbs was very concerned with the need to live our values in our everyday lives. We are called to honesty and integrity in our business dealings with each other.

They should not be seen as rivals or people whom we can exploit, but rather as sisters and brothers with whom we share the blessings of the Lord.

PRAYER. *Lord, may I be as generous and kind with others as You are with me.*

O NOT forget my teaching, but cherish my commandments in your heart.
—Prov 3:1

FEB. 4

REFLECTION. It is not enough to fulfill the commandments begrudgingly lest we do so with a sense of obligation and resentment. We are called to see the will of God as the most precious thing we can discover in our lives.

The psalms encourage us to reflect upon God's law both day and night.

PRAYER. *Teach me Your ways, O Lord, and guide me in Your paths.*

NTRUST everything that you do to the Lord, and your plans will turn out to be successful.
—Prov 16:3

FEB. 5

REFLECTION. St. Agatha entrusted everything she had and was to the Lord throughout her terrible sufferings in her martyrdom. Her persecutors could kill her, but they could never harm her.

Christians define "success" not by how much we have, but rather by how faithful we are in our witness to God's call.

PRAYER. *St. Agatha, please help me to give faithful witness to my beliefs.*

F YOU lose heart in time of adversity, your strength will indeed be limited. —Prov 24:10

FEB. 6

REFLECTION. St. Paul Miki and his companions displayed great courage and trust in the ways of the Lord as they were carried to their martyrdom. They were able to see God's plan in the midst of what others would have judged failure.

This is a daily challenge for each of us.

PRAYER. *St. Paul Miki, teach me to trust in the Lord, especially in times of difficulty.*

IKE a drop of water from the sea or a grain of sand, such are these few years compared with eternity. —Sir 18:10

FEB. 7

REFLECTION. Every once in a while, it is good to reflect upon the fact that life is short, while eternity knows no end.

This can be a good corrective for the way we view what we are doing and why we are doing it. We now live in time, but we were ultimately created for eternity.

PRAYER. *Lord, lead me from this place and time to Your eternal home.*

NEVER say, "I will do to him as he has done to me; I will pay him back for what he has done." —Prov 24:29

FEB. 8

REFLECTION. Although St. Josephine Bakita suffered terribly in her life, including having to endure the outrages of slavery, she was able to forgive and pray for those who had persecuted her and dedicate herself to a life of cheerful service to others.

She was especially known for her smile. Her difficulties never extinguished her spirit of joy.

PRAYER. *Lord Jesus, teach me to pray for those who make my life difficult.*

DO NOT boast about your elegant clothes or become proud when you receive honors. —Sir 11:4

FEB. 9

REFLECTION. The true value of a person is not based upon external circumstances, but rather upon the virtue of that person's heart. We see that in the choice of David instead of his brothers to be the king of Israel.

This requires a discernment on our part to judge others in the way that God would judge them.

PRAYER. *Let me see the inner beauty of those around me, Lord.*

B UY truth and do not sell it; this is wisdom, instruction, and understanding.

—Prov 23:23

FEB. 10

REFLECTION. Like St. Scholastica, we are called to discern the true values that God has placed in our lives and to be consistent in the way that we live them.

We need to seek guidance from God, listen to the advice of others, and reflect upon what we have heard and seen.

PRAYER. *May I discern Your call, O Lord, and follow wherever You might lead me.*

W HEN the good woman opens her mouth, wisdom issues forth, and on her tongue is kindly advice.

—Prov 31:26

FEB. 11

REFLECTION. The Blessed Virgin Mary, the Immaculate Conception, appeared to St. Bernadette Soubirous to call us to prayer and penance. She wanted to bring healing to our souls and our bodies.

Millions of people visit the Shrine in Lourdes each year to partake of the grace that Mary's presence and message offer.

PRAYER. *Our Lady of Lourdes, pray for us.*

O NOT say, "God is responsible for my falling astray," for you ought not do what he hates. —Sir 15:12

FEB. 12

REFLECTION. It is easy to blame our shortcomings on others, even on God. A good examination of conscience reminds us that we are responsible for what we have chosen to do.

This is why, when we go to the Sacrament of Reconciliation, we should confess our own sins and not the flaws of others.

PRAYER. *Lord, Jesus Christ, Son of the Living God, have mercy on me, a sinner.*

GIFT given secretly appeases anger. —Prov 21:14a

FEB. 13

REFLECTION. How can we bring healing to a situation in which someone is very angry at us. Secretly extending a sign of our regret, possibly by way of a small gift, can be a start to a healing of the situation.

This gift could be physical or it could be spiritual, such as praying for the person with whom we are having difficulty.

PRAYER. *Lord, please bless* ________ *and bring peace to our relationship.*

O NOT refrain from speaking at an opportune time, and do not conceal your wisdom. —Sir 4:23

FEB. 14

REFLECTION. Cyril and Methodius bravely traveled to pagan territory to share the Good News, even inventing an alphabet so that it could be presented in a way that the people would understand it.

What forms of truth could I share with those around me? How could I adapt its transmission so that others could embrace it?

PRAYER. *Saints Cyril and Methodius, pray for us.*

N THE beginning when God created man, he left him free to make his own decisions. —Sir 15:14

FEB. 15

REFLECTION. Is there anything that God cannot do? God cannot force us to love Him. This is why He gave us free will. God didn't want us to be slaves, but rather friends.

We can use that free will to say "yes" to God's call, or we can abuse it by rejecting God's invitation.

PRAYER. *Loving God, may I use my freedom to embrace You and Your call in my life.*

PROFUSION of dreams leads to excessive vanity. Therefore, fear God.

—Eccl 5:6

FEB. 16

REFLECTION. It is often difficult to know our limits. We all have dreams of what we could be, or own, or control.

Reflecting upon God reminds us that we are most of all called to be humble servants of God and of each other. Success is not measured by earthly standards, but rather by how well we conform to the Gospel.

PRAYER. *May my greatest desire be to serve You, God, and my neighbor.*

LL DAY long the godless continues to covet, whereas the righteous gives unsparingly.

—Prov 21:26

FEB. 17

REFLECTION. We can measure what we truly hold to be important in our lives by how we treat money and our other possessions.

Are they the goal of our life, or are they recognized as a gift from God that should be shared with those who most need our assistance?

PRAYER. *Teach me, O Lord, to be generous with all that I have received from You.*

O GOOD, no good," says the buyer, but then he goes forth to boast about his bargain. —Prov 20:14

FEB. 18

REFLECTION. Our Christian values should be seen even in the way that we do business. Rather than trying to gain an advantage over another, we should try to be honest and sincere in the way that we treat that person.

The Kingdom of God is based on cooperation and the mutual good rather than competition and selfishness.

PRAYER. *God, teach me to be as generous with my goods as You are with Your love.*

WO are better than one; they earn a far greater reward for their toil. —Eccl 4:9

FEB. 19

REFLECTION. We often think that it would be easier to do something on our own rather than ask another to help us.

But there is value in working with another. Not only do we accomplish what we were seeking to do, but we also build community by inviting others to participate in our projects.

PRAYER. *Jesus, teach me to reach out and to ask for help from those around me.*

RAIN a child in the way he should go, and he will not deviate from it, even in his old age. —Prov 22:6

FEB. 20

REFLECTION. One of the most important lessons we can share with our children is our Christian values. This is a lifelong gift to them.

This lesson has to be shared by word, but even more by the everyday example that we give with our own lives. Children can see right through hypocrisy.

PRAYER. *May I always live and share my Christian values with the little ones of the Lord.*

AVE you heard a rumor? Let it die with you; be assured, if you hold it in, it will not cause you to burst asunder. —Sir 19:10

FEB. 21

REFLECTION. Knowledge is power. This is why we often like to be the first one to share the latest juicy gossip with those around us.

Yet, silence might be a more charitable way to respond to a rumor. We don't need to say everything we think we know (and which might not even be true).

PRAYER. *Lord, teach me when to speak and when to keep silent.*

KING'S heart is like a stream of water in the hand of the Lord; he directs it wherever he pleases. —Prov 21:1

FEB. 22

REFLECTION. St. Peter and his successors were given authority over the whole Church. We see that when Jesus gave him the keys of the kingdom and when Jesus asked Peter three times if he loved Him and told him to watch over the sheep.

Do I pray for the Holy Father regularly and all the others who guide our Church?

PRAYER. *St. Peter, pray for us who are called to be Church.*

Y CHILD, when you come to serve the Lord, prepare yourself to endure trials. —Sir 2:1

FEB. 23

REFLECTION. There is a saying, "No good deed goes unpunished." If we try to do what is right, we will have to pay a price. We will have to fight the selfish impulses within our own hearts.

We will also have to have the courage to live and profess our values when that is unpopular and will cost us greatly.

PRAYER. *All you holy martyrs of the faith, pray for me.*

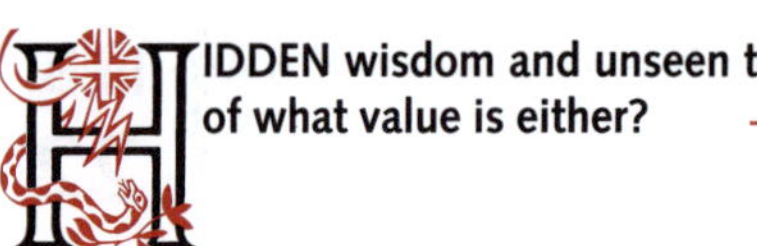

HIDDEN wisdom and unseen treasure— of what value is either? —Sir 20:30

FEB. 24

REFLECTION. Jesus spoke of the talents that have been given to us and how we should use them to serve the Kingdom instead of hiding them away.

Likewise, He spoke of putting our lamps on a stand where their light will illuminate the world. This is especially true of the wisdom God has poured into our hearts and minds.

PRAYER. *May I be willing to share my wisdom with others in word and deed.*

NEVER remove the ancient boundary stone that your ancestors set up. —Prov 22:28

FEB. 25

REFLECTION. In Israel, property was thought of as being a gift of God. To try to acquire it, especially through unjust means, was a sin against one's neighbor but also against God.

Do I view what I have as a gift from God, and do I respect what others have (their possessions, their reputation, etc.)?

PRAYER. *Thank You, Lord, for what I have, and thank You for what others have as well.*

OW much better it is to rebuke than to fume. —Sir 20:2

FEB. 26

REFLECTION. There are times when we decide to hold our anger in, but we do not get rid of it. Rather, it smolders in our hearts and eventually explodes in a way that can be very damaging.

It is much better to find a healthy way to express our anger so that we don't have to continue to carry around its burden.

PRAYER. *May I learn how to express my anger in the way that is most useful.*

HAVE seen everything that has been done under the sun, and behold all is vanity... —Eccl 1:14

FEB. 27

REFLECTION. Many of the things that we seek in life do not satisfy the deepest hunger of our hearts. They are more like a medicine which makes us feel better for a time, but they do not really cure the illness.

We have to ask ourselves honestly, "What is worth living for? What should be the source of my deepest yearning?"

PRAYER. *Lord, may I honestly evaluate what is most important in my life.*

THE man of gracious speech will have the king as a friend. —Prov 22:11b

FEB. 28

REFLECTION. If we speak with kindness, gentleness, and humility, people will want to be around us. They will sense the peace in our hearts and want to have that peace themselves.

If we are always angry and complaining, they will seek to avoid us. The last thing most people need is a friend who is filled with negativity.

PRAYER. *Lord, teach me what to say and when to say it.*

I KNOW that whatever God does endures forever; nothing can be added to it or subtracted from it. —Eccl 3:14

FEB. 29

REFLECTION. When I view the stars at night, or consider the changing of the seasons, or any of the other wonders that God has created, I feel a sense of awe.

It is already a great thing to know that God created these things, but even greater to know that He created them for me.

PRAYER. *Thank You, Lord, thank You for all the wonders of creation.*

OR everything there is a season, and a time for every activity under heaven.

—Eccl 3:1

MAR. 1

REFLECTION. Fighting against the patterns for life will only bring us frustration. Walking with God brings us a sense of profound peace.

This truth is based on the fact that God has a plan for each of us. We are not in charge—God is. Surrendering to God's Will is what brings us God's peace.

PRAYER. *God, may I find the meaning of peace, shalom, within the journey of my life.*

ONTROL yourself if you are given to overindulgence. —Prov 23:2

MAR. 2

REFLECTION. Discipline is a word that few of us like to hear, but it is essential in the spiritual life.

Following Christ means not only saying "yes" to His call; it also means saying "no" to those things which might distract us. This includes even good things which could become too important for us.

PRAYER. *Teach me, O Lord, Your discipline which leads to Your freedom.*

ANYONE who despises his neighbor is a sinner, but blessed is he who is kind to the poor. —Prov 14:21

MAR. 3

REFLECTION. Our faith is not only a question of having a vertical relationship with God. It also includes a horizontal dimension: our relationship with our neighbor.

Blessed is that person who can see the face of God in others (family, friends, acquaintances, and even strangers) for they were all created in God's image and likeness.

PRAYER. *May I never turn away anyone who needs my love and attention.*

MY CHILD, have you sinned? Do not sin anymore and ask forgiveness for your past sins. —Sir 21:1

MAR. 4

REFLECTION. The first step to true conversion is the recognition that we need God's forgiveness. This requires an act of vulnerability: acknowledging that we cannot do this alone.

The second step is to commit ourselves to stop sinning. This does not mean that we will have an automatic or complete success, but each day we must try a little harder.

PRAYER. *Have mercy on me, O God, for I have sinned.*

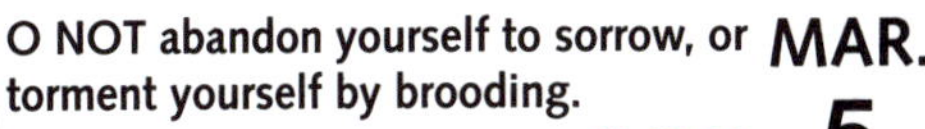

DO NOT abandon yourself to sorrow, or torment yourself by brooding.

—Sir 30:21

MAR. 5

REFLECTION. Our minds can torment us with things that could have gone better. Torturing ourselves with the "could have been" ideas does not really help us find joy.

What is, is. Now, what can I do to make things better? How can I use what has happened as a lesson on how to live better in the future?

PRAYER. *May I find peace with the past, O Lord, and commit myself to live in the present.*

LIKE apples of gold inlaid with silver are words that are aptly spoken. —Prov 25:11

MAR. 6

REFLECTION. Words have tremendous power. God created the universe using words. Words transform bread and wine into the body and blood of Christ. Kind words heal broken hearts.

We have the opportunity to build up the Kingdom each and every day by using words of kindness and compassion and gratitude and even contrition.

PRAYER. *O Lord, open my lips. And my mouth shall proclaim Your praise.*

E BRIEF but say much in a few words; convey the impression of knowledge but preferring to hold your tongue. —Sir 32:8

MAR. 7

REFLECTION. Some people talk on and on and never really say anything of value. Others do not say all that much, but what they do say is well worth hearing.

Exercising a certain prudence in how much we talk and what we say could make what we do say all the more valuable to those who hear it.

PRAYER. *Lord, teach me how to listen and ponder more than speak.*

IKE cold water to a thirsty throat is good news from a distant land. —Prov 25:25

MAR. 8

REFLECTION. Our world is filled with reports of bad news. We can be overwhelmed by what we see on TV or our computer screen.

Hearing about acts of charity, about peace being established, about children in need being fed and clothed are all things which can heal our sense of helplessness and hopelessness.

PRAYER. *Lord, let me hear about the good news of the world, the Good News of Your Kingdom.*

DO NOT forsake your friend or the friend of your father. —Prov 27:10a

MAR. 9

REFLECTION. We can become so busy with daily life that we might not find time for those who really count.

Sometimes, it is important to do a little less and spend more time with those who are important to us. We might even want to reach out to old friends of the family with whom we have lost contact.

PRAYER. *Lord, may I find truly good friends with whom I can share my life.*

ONE who is covetous will never be satisfied with money, nor will the lover of wealth be content with gain. —Eccl 5:9

MAR. 10

REFLECTION. We can easily want more and more in our lives. We must ask ourselves whether all that we possess (money, clothes, prestige, etc.) really brings us a profound sense of joy.

An alternative approach would be to view what we have been given as a gift from God, a gift which is to be shared with those who are in need.

PRAYER. *Lord, may I never allow my possessions to possess me.*

FOOL laughs at the top of his voice, but a prudent man smiles quietly.
—Sir 21:20

MAR. 11

REFLECTION. It is usually imprudent to make a show of ourselves in front of others. This is often an attempt to make ourselves the center of attention.

It would be better to join in the celebration in a quiet and dignified manner. We can enjoy the party without making a clown of ourselves.

PRAYER. *May my joys be true joys and not merely moments of foolish excess.*

O NOT waste your words on a fool who will only despise the wisdom of your comments.
—Prov 23:9

MAR. 12

REFLECTION. There is a time to recognize that no matter what we say, it will not make any difference. Either the person is closed to correction, or possibly is simply not ready yet to hear it.

In those moments, we can interiorize our words as prayers offered up so that that person might someday be ready to listen.

PRAYER. *God, I pray for ____who needs to hear some things but is not ready to listen to them yet.*

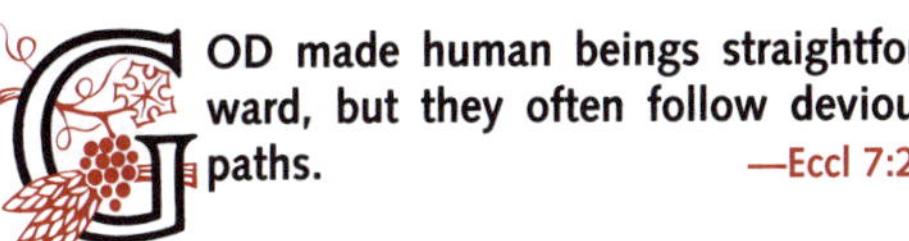

GOD made human beings straightforward, but they often follow devious paths. —Eccl 7:29

MAR. 13

REFLECTION. It is often difficult to sort out the hidden motives of what others do, and at times even to sort out the profound motives of what we do.

One of the goals of the spiritual life is to arrive at simplicity so that what we think and say and do might be consistent with what we believe.

PRAYER. *Purify my motives, Loving God, so that I might be a person of integrity.*

DIVINATIONS, omens, and dreams are all unreal; the mind portrays what you already expect. —Sir 34:5

MAR. 14

REFLECTION. Trying to discern the future by consulting horoscopes or psychics or using other such means is a waste of time.

God is in charge of our future, and God only reveals it slowly at the proper time. This is where trust comes in: to believe that no matter what happens God will be there for us.

PRAYER. *As the future unfolds, may I continue to trust in Your providence.*

O NOT push yourself forward in the king's presence or take a place where the great assemble. —Prov 25:6

MAR. 15

REFLECTION. Jesus said that when we come to a banquet, we should take the lowest place at table. We are not called to be famous or popular, but rather to be simple and humble.

Jesus came into the world to serve and not to be served, and if we want to be one of His disciples, we must try to do the same.

PRAYER. *Purify me of my overriding ambition, O Lord, and teach me to be humble.*

MIND based on intelligent reflection is like fine decoration on a smooth wall. —Sir 22:17

MAR. 16

REFLECTION. It is a true joy to deal with a person who has thought through things both logically and in the Lord. One senses that there are no hidden motives, no failure to communicate what the person really thinks.

This requires time and silence so that we might listen carefully to the voice of the Spirit speaking in our hearts.

PRAYER. *Speak, Lord, for Your servant is listening.*

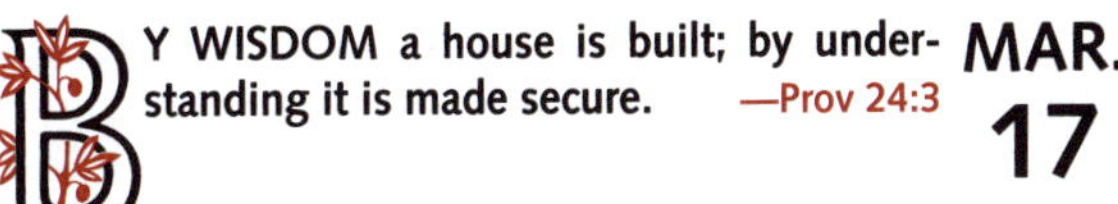
BY WISDOM a house is built; by understanding it is made secure. —Prov 24:3

MAR. 17

REFLECTION. St. Patrick spent most of his lifetime trying to build up the Church in Ireland. In doing this, he always let himself be led by the Wisdom of God.

Furthermore, understanding the truths of the faith as well as the needs of the people to whom he was preaching, he laid the Church upon a firm foundation.

PRAYER. *St. Patrick, pray for us and for the people of Ireland.*

A PATIENT man endures difficulties for a time, and then he regains his sense of contentment. —Sir 1:23

MAR. 18

REFLECTION. Every person will face difficulties in life. How we deal with those difficulties and how we let them affect us makes all the difference.

Patience is not ignoring the difficulty. Rather, it is a recognition that at this moment we cannot do a lot about it. The time will come when things will get better.

PRAYER. *Grant me patience, O Lord, with others, with difficulties, and especially with myself.*

LESSED is the one whose conscience does not reproach him and who has never lost hope. —Sir 14:2

MAR. 19

REFLECTION. The life of St. Joseph was filled with hard work and some difficult and dangerous times, yet he never lost hope. This was true even when he discovered that his fiancée, the Blessed Virgin Mary, was pregnant.

Rather, he listened to the voice of the Lord and showed both obedience to God and compassion toward Mary and her Child.

PRAYER. *St. Joseph, pray for us.*

HEN we eat and drink and find satisfaction in all our labors, this is a gift from God. —Eccl 3:13

MAR. 20

REFLECTION. What does it take for us to feel that things are going well in our life? It is often the simple pleasures that give the greatest comfort.

If we were to consider all the everyday joys for which we should be grateful, we would be filled with an overwhelming sense of gratitude and contentment.

PRAYER. *Give us, O Lord, our daily bread.*

HE netherworld and the abyss are never satisfied; the same is true of human eyes.
—Prov 27:20

MAR. 21

REFLECTION. The ancients believed that the netherworld was constantly seeking more and more people to devour. It would never be satisfied.

That is what our desires could resemble if we are not careful. It is good to examine our lives every so often and decide what we truly need and what is in excess.

PRAYER. *Grant me the grace to be able to distinguish what I want from what I need.*

HE bread of charity is life itself to the poor; whoever deprives them of it is a murderer.
—Sir 34:25

MAR. 22

REFLECTION. We can easily underestimate the importance of our acts of charity toward the poor. For them, it can make all the difference.

Besides giving money or food or clothing to some charitable organization, we should also consider spending time with someone who is poor and treating that person with dignity.

PRAYER. *Lord, may I consider every poor person to be my sister or my brother.*

OMEONE guilty of murder will be a fugitive till death. —Prov 28:17a

MAR. 23

REFLECTION. There are things that we do which will haunt us for the rest of our lives. We wonder how we could ever be forgiven for them.

Yet, Jesus, in the Sacrament of Reconciliation, promises to forgive everything that we have done. God's mercy and compassion are much greater than our guilt.

PRAYER. *Forgive me, Lord, for I have sinned.*

O NOT consort with drunkards or be one of those who gorge themselves with meat. —Prov 23:20

MAR. 24

REFLECTION. There is a natural human tendency to overdo it. Yet, whether this be food or drink or possessions or sex, it will always get us into trouble.

God's gifts are to be used with respect and not abused. We have to remember to say "no" to those things which would rob us of our dignity.

PRAYER. *May I use everything You have given me with respect and self-control.*

HE fear of the Lord provides instruction in wisdom, and to be humble is the way to honor. —Prov 15:33

MAR. 25

REFLECTION. There are few scenes in the Bible which show humility as well as Mary's surrender to the Will of God during the Annunciation.

She calls herself a handmaid of the Lord and she asks that God's Will be done. It is through this surrender that Jesus becomes incarnate in the world.

PRAYER. *Let it be done to me according to Your Word.*

O NOT allow your mouth to lead you into sin and then plead before God's messenger that it was all a mistake. —Eccl 5:5

MAR. 26

REFLECTION. We often seek to excuse away our faults when we are caught in them. I didn't mean to do it; I was confused; it seemed like the best thing to do, etc.

We cannot hope to find true conversion until we take responsibility for what we have done and admit that we are guilty and in need of God's mercy.

PRAYER. *Have mercy on me, O God, for I am a sinner.*

O NOT offer God a bribe, for he will not accept it. —Sir 35:14

MAR. 27

REFLECTION. Our prayers are sometimes forms of bribery: if You do this for me, then I will do this for You. It is almost as if our relationship with God were a question of commerce.

True prayer is honest dialog with God Who only wants what is best for us.

PRAYER. *Your Kingdom come, Your Will be done, on earth as it is in heaven.*

E WHO chases fantasies will live in poverty. —Prov 28:19b

MAR. 28

REFLECTION. It is often tempting to escape into an unreal world of things that could be or could have been. This day dreaming doesn't really help improve our situation.

We need to sit down and be brutally honest with ourselves about what concrete steps are needed to make things better.

PRAYER. *Lord, today I promise to do the following: ________.*

OUR own conscience will sometimes give you a more accurate warning than seven watchmen stationed on a high tower. —Sir 37:14

MAR. 29

REFLECTION. Deep down, we know whether what we have done was good or bad. We have to listen to that small voice that helps us sort things out.

This means, however, that we have to work at forming our consciences so that they truly help us to live the ways of the Lord every day.

PRAYER. *Lord, never let me wander from Your path of truth and good.*

F I have too much, I may deny you and say, "Who is the Lord?" —Prov 30:9a

MAR. 30

REFLECTION. It seems strange to be worried about having too much, but abundance can be a danger. It can make us self-sufficient. We become our own gods.

A healthier way to judge the situation is to ask ourselves if there are things which we can afford to share with those who do not have enough.

PRAYER. *May I never forget that all that I have is a gift of Your Providence, O Lord.*

HEN the righteous triumph, there is a great celebration, but when the wicked prevail, the people go into hiding. —Prov 28:12

MAR. 31

REFLECTION. We all hope that good will win in the end. When it does not turn out that way, we are often very troubled.

It is important to remember that even when all seems lost, we can follow the example of Jesus dying on the Cross by choosing love and not hate.

PRAYER. *May Your Kingdom triumph upon the earth, O Lord, and may Your love prevail.*

AVE regard for your name for it will outlive you far longer than a thousand hoards of gold. —Sir 41:12

APR. 1

REFLECTION. The ancients were not sure of what happened in the afterlife, so they clung to the need to pass down a good name.

While our ideas about what comes after death are clearer, it is nevertheless good to have lived in such a way that we will have been a good example to those who follow us.

PRAYER. *May I live in such a way that I draw others to You, Lord.*

T IS better to pay heed to the rebuke of the wise than to listen to the songs of fools.

—Eccl 7:5

APR. 2

REFLECTION. All of us occasionally need to be corrected for what we are doing. Yet, it can be difficult to accept that correction without becoming defensive.

True humility recognizes that the words of a wise person are meant for our good and it makes us grateful that someone cares enough about us to intervene on our behalf.

PRAYER. *May I be humble enough to take seriously any corrections that I might receive.*

INE and music gladden the heart, but better than either is the love of wisdom.

—Sir 40:20

APR. 3

REFLECTION. It is good to celebrate every once in a while, but ultimately that will not bring us lasting joy.

Only Wisdom can bring us a joy that does not pass away. Wisdom is seeing things through the eyes of God. Wisdom is being where we know that God wants us to be.

PRAYER. *Teach me, Lord, Your ways of Wisdom.*

HEN anyone turns a deaf ear to the law, even his prayer is detestable.

—Prov 28:9

APR. 4

REFLECTION. This proverb is speaking about living in the law of God. If one chooses to live according to one's own whim, then this will lead to disaster.

How can we expect God to listen to our prayers when we have shut our ears to His call to live in His ways?

PRAYER. *Guide me in Your ways, O Lord, and teach me Your law of love.*

OT everything is good for everyone, nor do we all enjoy the same things.

—Sir 37:28

APR. 5

REFLECTION. We are all made with different desires and different goals. Each person has been given personal gifts to use for the common good.

This is why we must be careful not to impose our standards upon others, nor condemn ourselves for being different from them. Each of us is unique.

PRAYER. *Praise be to You, O Lord, for having created us in all of our diversity.*

AR better is a friend nearby than a brother who is far away. —Prov 27:10

APR. 6

REFLECTION. Jesus asked His disciples who His true mother and brother and sister are. It is those who chose to be one with Him.

Likewise, those people who share our joys and stick with us in our difficulties can often be more significant to us than our own blood relatives.

PRAYER. *Lord, grant me true friends, and let me be a true friend to them.*

NVY and anger shorten one's life, and anxiety brings on premature old age. —Sir 30:24

APR. 7

REFLECTION. Negative emotions can have a profound effect not only on our mental health but also our physical well-being.

If we suffer from envy and anger and anxiety, we must find a way to deal with them and seek healing (in the Lord, in spiritual direction, in counseling, etc.).

PRAYER. *Heal me, O Lord, of those tendencies to be overly negative and angry.*

HE quiet words of the wise are more to be heeded than the shouts of a ruler of fools. —Eccl 9:17

APR. 8

REFLECTION. How can we bring others around to understand what we are trying to share with them? Using aggressive language only creates a barrier between us and does not really resolve the problem.

Thinking and praying through our intervention can be much more useful. We have to learn to share our insights in a gentler and more respectful manner.

PRAYER. *May Your Holy Spirit speak in and through me, O Lord.*

ET another praise you, and not your own mouth. —Prov 27:2

APR. 9

REFLECTION. We do not have to make ourselves the hero of all of our stories. People tend to cringe when they hear us constantly talking about ourselves and our adventures.

Rather than praising ourselves, we could take the opportunity to recognize the good that others have done and speak about that.

PRAYER. *Thank You, Lord, for____ who has given me a good example.*

E PATIENT with someone in humble circumstances, and do not keep him waiting for his alms. —Sir 29:8

APR. 10

REFLECTION. Not everyone is capable of the same things. Some have great abilities and abundant circumstances; others are much less blessed.

We should be like God Who only expects from each person what that person can do. God judges us not according to what we "should" do, but rather according to what we "can" do.

PRAYER. *May I not expect more from others than that of which they are capable.*

HE stone comes back on the one who rolls it. —Prov 26:27

APR. 11

REFLECTION. There is a rabbinic saying, "as the sin, so the punishment." When we sin against another, we are the ones who get hurt most.

Sin pushes others away, and we find ourselves lonelier and more isolated. The only way to break the power of sin is to choose to love and thereby heal the wounds in our relationships.

PRAYER. *Lord, make me an instrument of Your peace. Where there is hatred, let me sow love.*

HE fear of the Lord surpasses everything; to whom can we compare the one who possesses it? —Sir 25:11

APR. 12

REFLECTION. A person who walks in the ways of the Lord recognizes God's presence in everyone and everything that person encounters. That person is a beacon of truth and peace.

Others will recognize that there is something special about him or her, and they will want to acquire what that person has found.

PRAYER. *Fill me with Your presence, Lord, so that I might help others to experience Your love.*

EVER be in a hurry to speak or hastily make a promise to God. —Eccl 5:1

APR. 13

REFLECTION. When we make resolutions on New Year's Day or at the beginning of Lent, we often over-promise, saying that we will do things which will simply not happen.

It is better to take stock and make reasonable commitments to the Lord (and to ourselves) in terms of how we will try to be more faithful in our discipleship.

PRAYER. *May I do that which I say, and may I be that which I am called to be.*

HE whispers of a gossiper are tasty morsels that corrode one's inner being. —Prov 26:22

APR. 14

REFLECTION. All of us like to hear that latest piece of juicy gossip, but we should ask ourselves if listening to those things or sharing them with others really makes us into better people.

There is a rule of thumb to recognize gossip: is it true, is it kind, and is it helpful.

PRAYER. *Let my words always be true, kind, and helpful, Lord.*

EEP for the dead man, for he has taken leave of the light. Weep for the fool, for he has taken leave of his wits. —Sir 22:11

APR. 15

REFLECTION. Which is worse: that a person dies, or that the common sense and wisdom in a person die?

In the first case, the person who dies is in the hands of the Lord, which is not a bad thing. In the second case, that person chooses foolishness and has turned his back on the Lord.

PRAYER. *Keep me from making foolish decisions and living in a way that rejects Your wisdom.*

F YOUR enemy is hungry, give him something to eat. —Prov 25:21 **APR. 16**

REFLECTION. When Jesus was nailed to the Cross, He forgave those who were persecuting Him. He saw the brokenness of His enemies and wanted to heal it.

Likewise, when we are kind and compassionate to those who have hurt us, we are showing them the love with which God loves them.

PRAYER. *I lift up to You, Lord, ____, with whom I am having difficulties.*

ETTER is a poor but wise youth than an old and foolish king who will no longer take advice. —Eccl 4:13 **APR. 17**

REFLECTION. What is the best life that we can live? It is not that we have an abundance of whatever we want.

Rather, the best we can hope for is to be wise. That is what makes life meaningful, and it is what fills us with a sense of peace and accomplishment.

PRAYER. *Grant me Wisdom, the attendant at Your throne.*

T IS better to serve the Lord while awaiting the inevitable than to be an ignorant helmsman of one's own life. —Sir 20:32

APR. 18

REFLECTION. We like to think that we are in charge of our own destiny, but this is not the case.

God has given us free will to work with Him to create our future. It is not all God, nor is it all us. God has given us so much dignity that He makes us His partners in this process.

PRAYER. *May I commit myself to my responsibility and respect Your role in shaping my future.*

O NOT enter too frequently into your neighbor's house lest he become tired of you and begins to hate you. —Prov 25:17

APR. 19

REFLECTION. We have to recognize and respect boundaries in people's lives. It is good to reach out to others in friendship, but it is also good to recognize when it is time to go home and give them some space.

Being their friend does not mean we are free to hold them hostage to our own needs.

PRAYER. *Teach me when to reach out and when to pull back out of respect for others.*

HE prayer of the poor man goes from his lips straight to the ear of God, and justice is speedily granted him.

—Sir 21:5

APR. 20

REFLECTION. It is not that God loves the poor more than the rich, but rather God responds to each of us as we most need.

The rich person can often take care of his own needs, while the poor person has no one else upon whom he can place his hopes other than God.

PRAYER. *Lord, please always be with those who need You most.*

ISDOM is far more valuable than silver, and her revenue is greater than that of gold. **—Prov 3:14**

APR. 21

REFLECTION. What is the greatest treasure that we could accrue? It is not gold or silver, riches or fame or privilege.

Our greatest treasure is Wisdom, for through it we can see the wonders of God's goodness and work to make this world a better place, the place that God always intended it to be.

PRAYER. *Let me choose my treasure carefully, always holding on to that which lasts into eternity.*

EAT honey, my son, for it is good, and the drippings of the honeycomb are sweet to the taste. —Prov 24:13

APR. 22

REFLECTION. This proverb is not just about honey for the next verse says that wisdom is sweeter and more pleasing than honey.

We can often consider the good things around us and see them as something that points to a greater reality. All of creation points to our good and gracious God.

PRAYER. *May I see Your goodness, Lord, in the everyday events of my life.*

GOD will judge both the righteous and the wicked, for he has appointed a time for every matter. —Eccl 3:17

APR. 23

REFLECTION. God is very patient and gives us time to change our ways. But sooner or later, there is a time of reckoning for how we have lived.

It would be good if we were to find out that the end of the world was at hand, and we could say that we have always been ready for it.

PRAYER. *May I live each day as if it were my first day, my last day, my only day.*

EVER make friends with a man prone to anger, and do not associate with anyone who is wrathful. —Prov 22:24

APR. 24

REFLECTION. While we should love everyone with the love with which God loves them, there are certain people whom we have to love from a distance.

Whether because of their temperament or our weakness, these people bring out the worst in us. It is best to recognize this and to deal with them at arm's length.

PRAYER. *Lord, I do not know how to respond to____. Teach me how to deal with this person.*

O MATTER how much we say, our words will never prove adequate; to sum it all up, "He is the all!" —Sir 43:27

APR. 25

REFLECTION. St. Mark was probably the first evangelist to write an account of the life and ministry of Jesus. He is said to have received much of his material from St. Peter.

In Mark's Gospel, Jesus is proclaimed as the Son of God when He is on the Cross for that is when we most clearly see how much God loves us.

PRAYER. *Jesus, my Lord and my God, my God and my All.*

COARSE person is like an indiscreet story that is continually on the lips of the ignorant. —Sir 20:19

APR. 26

REFLECTION. A crude person can often be the life of the party, but that person leaves everyone feeling a bit uncomfortable and even somehow unclean.

We choose to be well mannered and discrete not only because it shows us to be worthwhile, but also because it shows respect toward those around us.

PRAYER. *May I respect those around me enough to treat them with good manners.*

HOEVER craves pleasure will end up in want; whoever loves wine and oil will never grow rich. —Prov 21:17

APR. 27

REFLECTION. God did not create us to have a good time. God created us to be His image and likeness.

When God reveals what it means to be God-like in His Only Son, it is in terms of service and compassion. We are most like Jesus when we view everyone around us as people whom we should serve.

PRAYER. *Teach me to serve You, O Lord, in the people around me.*

SOMETIMES a word is better than an expensive gift, both are the hallmark of a gracious person. —Sir 18:17

APR. 28

REFLECTION. A kind word, a compliment, a compassionate remark can truly make a person's day. Like God, we have the power to create with our words and to destroy.

Simply treating others with respect, especially those who don't think they deserve it and often don't respect themselves, can bring healing to that person.

PRAYER. *Lord, may I sow hope where there is despair and where there is sadness, joy.*

YOU who are simple, acquire prudence; you who are foolish, acquire understanding. —Prov 8:5

APR. 29

REFLECTION. St. Catherine of Siena dedicated herself to prayer and contemplation. Yet, she never used this as an escape from everyday life.

She was in communication with many of the leaders of her day, including the Pope, giving them advice on how they should rule in a way that would bring people closer to the Lord.

PRAYER. *St. Catherine of Siena, pray for us.*

EFORE each man are life and death, and whichever one he chooses will be given. —Sir 15:17

APR. 30

REFLECTION. God has given us a choice: we can choose to follow in His ways and be filled with His life, or we can choose to reject His message and choose death.

God does not want to send anyone to Hell, but God also does not want to force us to love Him. We have to choose the path to life eternal.

PRAYER. *Send Your Holy Spirit into my heart, O Lord, so that I might choose the path to life.*

IVE me neither poverty nor riches, but simply provide me with the food that I need. —Prov 30:8bc

MAY 1

REFLECTION. St. Joseph, whose feast we celebrate today under the title of St. Joseph the Worker, struggled to earn a living for his family as a carpenter (not considered to be the best of occupations in his days).

His fame comes not from the tremendous deeds he did, but from his daily, conscientious dedication to his tasks.

PRAYER. *St. Joseph the Worker, pray for me.*

CQUIRE wisdom and no matter what the cost, acquire understanding.

—Prov 4:7

MAY 2

REFLECTION. Wisdom is being able to see things from God's point of view. Understanding is having the everyday knowledge in order to do things well.

Both are needed. Wisdom is more theoretical, and it involves the heart and mind. Understanding is more practical, and it involves the work of our hands and the sweat of our brow.

PRAYER. *Lord, grant me Your Wisdom from on high as well as Your practical understanding.*

OD is a shield to those who trust in him.

—Prov 30:5b

MAY 3

REFLECTION. Saints Philip and James were two apostles who proclaimed the Word in the countries to the east of Israel. They were martyred there.

The proclamation of the Gospel in word and deed always carries a price. The apostles considered their suffering to be a privilege and a sharing in the Passion of Christ.

PRAYER. *Saints Philip and James, pray for us.*

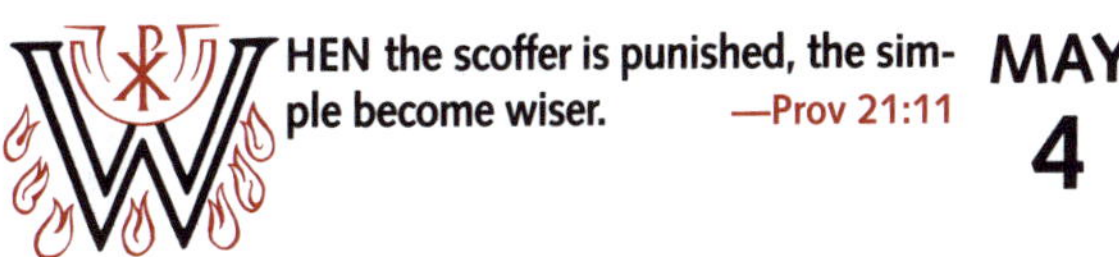

WHEN the scoffer is punished, the simple become wiser. —Prov 21:11

MAY 4

REFLECTION. There are times when we have to have the courage to tell certain people that what they are saying is inappropriate and unkind.

If we were not to do this, then innocent and simple people might easily buy into their message and adopt some of their mistaken attitudes.

PRAYER. *Lord, give me the courage to speak up when it is appropriate and needed.*

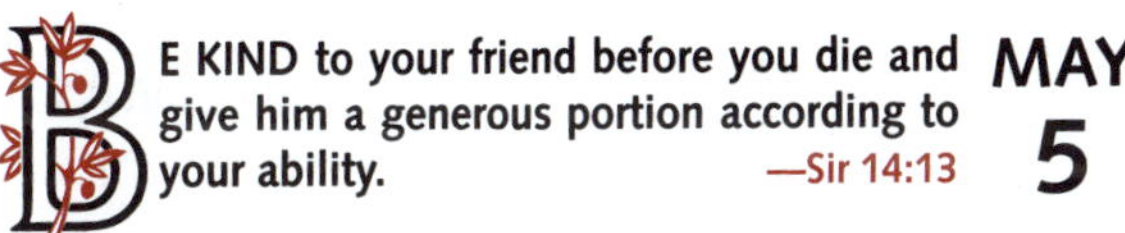

BE KIND to your friend before you die and give him a generous portion according to your ability. —Sir 14:13

MAY 5

REFLECTION. We don't really know how much time we have in this life. Today is the day that we should share our time and talent with those who are most important to us.

It is sad to be at a funeral home and hear people say, "I wish I would have done this or that, but now it is too late."

PRAYER. *Lord, may I do as much good as I can for as long as You give me.*

A PERSON'S ways may seem right to him, but the Lord weighs the heart.

—Prov 21:2

MAY 6

REFLECTION. It is easy to delude ourselves, thinking that everything that we are doing is correct and just.

Yet, there are hidden motivations in all of our hearts (hidden even from ourselves). We need the help of the Lord to sort out those intentions and to purify them in God's love and generosity.

PRAYER. *Lord, You alone truly know my heart. Purify my intentions to conform them to Your Will.*

DO NOT say, "I am self-sufficient; what harm can come to me now?"

—Sir 11:24

MAY 7

REFLECTION. We all like to do things on our own, and one of our greatest fears is that we will one day be totally dependent upon others.

Asking others for help, even now, is a good lesson in how interdependent we already are. Placing our life in God's hands is a good reminder of how we depend upon God for everything.

PRAYER. *Lord, may I not be so proud that I cannot ask others and You for help.*

EIGHTS and measures that are not consistent are an abomination to the Lord. —Prov 20:10

MAY 8

REFLECTION. While it was important to be clever in the ancient world (even Jesus spoke about being clever in spiritual matters), it was not considered right to be crafty.

Our business dealings should reflect the values we hold as Christians. We should not try to get as much as possible from the other, but rather treat that person fairly.

PRAYER. *May my dealings with others reflect my respect for them.*

NE who finds a wife finds happiness and receives favor from the Lord. —Prov 18:22

MAY 9

REFLECTION. While this proverb is stated from a male point of view, it holds true for both sides. Finding a good husband or wife is a true blessing.

But that relationship must be cared for every day or else it could degenerate into an agreement to live together but without a commitment of love.

PRAYER. *Lord, bless those who are married, especially those whose marriage is in difficulty.*

O NOT find fault before checking out the evidence; examine first, and then criticize. —Sir 11:7

MAY 10

REFLECTION. Some people have a tendency to be critical of others even before they know all of the facts. They approach situations with a prejudicial attitude.

We have to give people the benefit of a doubt and truly try to understand why something is being done the way that it is being done.

PRAYER. *May I always try to understand before I criticize.*

OR what does a person gain from all the toil and effort that he has expended under the sun? —Eccl 2:22

MAY 11

REFLECTION. The book of Ecclesiastes speaks over and over again of how we work so hard for things that do not last in the long run.

Jesus spoke about building up treasures in heaven. If we commit ourselves to working for the Kingdom (in our relationship with God and neighbor, in word and deed), then we will have established something worthwhile.

PRAYER. *Your Kingdom come, Your will be done, on earth as it is in heaven.*

DO NOT engage in arguing about something that does not concern you.

—Sir 11:9

MAY 12

REFLECTION. It is so easy to get caught up in an argument that has nothing to do with us. This is often a waste of time and energy.

That doesn't mean that we shouldn't help those we love or who need our help, but we have to be prudent in how much we get involved in other people's business.

PRAYER. *Lord, may I be a person of peace and not of discord.*

FEAR God and keep his commandments, for that is the responsibility of everyone.

—Eccl 12:13

MAY 13

REFLECTION. When Our Lady appeared to three small children at Fatima, she called upon all believers in the world to turn their hearts to her Son.

This is a clear sign that this was truly a message from Mary. In her authentic apparitions, she always speaks of her Son and of our duty to obey Him.

PRAYER. *Our Lady of Fatima, pray for us.*

HE lot is cast into the lap, but the decision comes from the Lord. —Prov 16:33

MAY 14

REFLECTION. When Judas Iscariot killed himself, the apostles chose another disciple to take his place as an apostle.

They chose two candidates, but then decided between them by lot so that the final decision would be made by the Holy Spirit and not themselves. This reminds us that we have to invite the Spirit into all of our decisions.

PRAYER. *St. Matthias the Apostle, pray for us.*

O NOT praise anyone for his good looks or despise any on the basis of his appearance. —Sir 11:2

MAY 15

REFLECTION. There is a saying that beauty is only skin deep. What is truly important is the character of a person.

Yet, our society has glorified physical beauty and youth so much that we can fall into the trap of judging ourselves and others by looks. We have to remember that in God's eyes we and they are all beautiful.

PRAYER. *Lord, let me recognize the beauty of each person whom I meet.*

NYONE who is lazy in his work is a brother to the one who wages destruction.
—Prov 18:9

MAY 16

REFLECTION. We might think that being lazy is a neutral stance, that we don't really hurt anyone else.

But this proverb reminds us that laziness is a form of theft. We are robbing God and others of what we could have done. We should remember the fate of the servant in the Gospels who failed to invest his master's talents.

PRAYER. *Lord, give me the energy and enthusiasm to do what needs to be done.*

HE fear of the Lord is the beginning of acceptance, while stubbornness and pride are the beginning of rejection.
—Sir 10:21

MAY 17

REFLECTION. When we recognize that God is in charge, we find a sense of peace. We realize that while we can pray to God to remedy the situation, ultimately God will decide what is best for us.

When we keep trying to control the situation, we end up being resentful and frustrated.

PRAYER. *Into Your hands, O Lord, I entrust my spirit.*

HE whispers of a gossiper are tasty morsels that corrode one's inner being.
—Prov 18:8

MAY 18

REFLECTION. The little pieces of gossip that we hear or share can seem to be entertaining and harmless, but they can have a damaging effect.

They hurt the people about whom we are talking, for they have no way to defend themselves. They hurt us, for it means that we are willing to hurt others for our own amusement.

PRAYER. *Lord, may I treat every person with the profound respect that person deserves.*

S DREAMS come when there are many cares, so does the speech of a fool when there are many words. —Eccl 5:2

MAY 19

REFLECTION. It is easy to slip into escapism when we face difficulties. That might be with our dreams, or even with our endless and pointless words.

It is more useful to evaluate the situation honestly and then commit ourselves to the best course of action, which sometimes means doing something positive, and at other times accepting our fate.

PRAYER. *Lord, please don't let me waste my time on strategies that will not do any good.*

ISDOM cries out in the street; she raises her voice in the public squares. —Prov 1:20

MAY 20

REFLECTION. St. Bernardine of Siena was famous for his preaching ministry. He would attract thousands who wanted to hear him speak and who wanted to go to confession.

When is the last time that I went to a religious talk or made a retreat or went to a Shrine? Maybe I need that spiritual shot in the arm.

PRAYER. *St. Bernardine of Siena, pray for us.*

LENGTHY illness baffles the doctor; the king of today will be a corpse tomorrow. —Sir 10:10

MAY 21

REFLECTION. We do not know how much longer we have to live.

We have to use each minute of our lives as a precious gift. Like St. Paul, we have to embrace life while it lasts, but also be ready to embrace death when it comes to take us home to our Lord.

PRAYER. *Lord, may I live my life to the fullest and may I embrace death peacefully.*

F YOU do good, know for whom you are doing it, and your good deeds will have their desired effect. —Sir 12:1

MAY 22

REFLECTION. When we help those in need, we are helping that person but we are also serving the Lord.

Remember what Jesus said when He separated the sheep from the goats in the final judgment: "As often as you did it for the least of My brethren, you did it for Me."

PRAYER. *May I see Your face in the face of everyone whom I am called to help.*

VEN a fool who keeps silent is considered wise. —Prov 17:28

MAY 23

REFLECTION. It is a great gift to know that we don't know. We don't have to offer opinions or insights into things about which we know nothing.

Sometimes wisdom is expressed not in what we say, but in the fact that we have the courage to admit that we don't have anything to say about an issue.

PRAYER. *May I be wise in what I say and in what I don't say.*

LL one's toil is for the mouth, yet his appetite is never satisfied. —Eccl 6:7

MAY 24

REFLECTION. We work hard to make a living, but we are often tempted to want more and more and more.

We have to ask ourselves, "when is what I have enough?" Can I be satisfied with having less, but having more time and energy to be with the people I really love?

PRAYER. *Lord, teach me not to want more than I need.*

ISDOM is designed to enable people to appreciate wisdom and discipline and to comprehend words that foster insight. —Prov 1:2

MAY 25

REFLECTION. St. Bede was a great scholar in the early Middle Ages. He wrote a history to speak of the conversion of the Anglo-Saxons to Christianity.

It is good to remember our past and to share those stories. It is through salvation history (the history of Israel but also our personal salvation history) that God reveals His plan.

PRAYER. *St. Bede the Venerable, pray for us.*

MAN'S wisdom lights up his face, softening the hardness of his countenance.
—Eccl 8:1

MAY 26

REFLECTION. People can read our intentions upon our faces. If we approach others with a kind and gentle face, one that speaks of our acceptance of them, then they will sense the goodness we hold for them.

If we walk around with a frown on our faces, then they will know that we hold them in disregard.

PRAYER. *May my face be a beacon of hope for those whom I encounter.*

CHEERFUL heart is excellent medicine, but a crushed spirit dries up the bones.
—Prov 17:22

MAY 27

REFLECTION. When things are going well, we often feel good and uplifted. When things are not going well, our spirit crashes to the ground.

How can I share both my joys and my grief with the Lord and with those around me? How can I use both to reach out to others instead of closing in on myself.

PRAYER. *Lord, be with me when I laugh and when I cry.*

NEW friend is like new wine; only when it has sufficiently aged can you drink it with pleasure. —Sir 9:10

MAY 28

REFLECTION. We have to be careful when new people enter our lives. We should welcome them, but we should be cautious about trusting them too much until we really know them.

Some people are not mature or constant enough to become a true friend. We should not place that responsibility on them if they can't carry that load.

PRAYER. *Lord, teach me to be a good friend to those around me.*

O NOT assert that the past was better than the present, for such a statement is not a sign of wisdom. —Eccl 7:10

MAY 29

REFLECTION. The past was not all good, and the present and future do not possess the solution to every problem.

We have to use what is good from the past and not abandon it, but we also have to be ready to embrace what is new as we work toward creating the future.

PRAYER. *Lord, the past, present, and future belong to You, for You are the Alpha and the Omega.*

RIDE goes before disaster, and a haughty spirit goes before a fall. —Prov 16:18

MAY 30

REFLECTION. When we are filled with pride and are arrogant, we will sooner or later face the consequences of our attitude.

People will distance themselves from us for they will not want to be abused by our pushiness, and when we eventually make a mistake, some of them will rejoice in our fall.

PRAYER. *Teach me humility, Lord, and help me to embrace simplicity.*

ING with all your heart and voice and bless the name of God. —Sir 39:35

MAY 31

REFLECTION. Elizabeth, the mother of John the Baptist, rejoiced at the arrival of Mary during the Visitation.

Mary celebrated her greeting and the wonders the Lord had worked through them with a canticle of joy which we call the Magnificat in which she announced, "My soul proclaims the greatness of the Lord."

PRAYER. *May my spirit always rejoice in God, my maker.*

LANS miscarry when counsel is lacking, but they succeed when there are many counselors. —Prov 15:22

JUNE 1

REFLECTION. It is always good to get the opinions of those around us. We could easily blind ourselves from seeing the situation as it is because of what we would like to see or do.

This, of course, includes laying our plans before the Lord and looking at things through the eyes of God.

PRAYER. *Open my ears, Lord, to hear the wise counsel of those around me.*

ETTER a dish of herbs served with love than a fattened ox accompanied by hatred. —Prov 15:17

JUNE 2

REFLECTION. The externals are most often not as important as the interior disposition. If there is love in a family (or any group of people), then there will be joy in the humblest of circumstances.

If, however, there is rancor, then no matter how beautiful and magnificent things seem to be on the surface, there will be no peace or contentment.

PRAYER. *Lord, send peace into my heart and the hearts of those around me.*

Y SON, if sinners try to entice you, refuse to join them. —Prov 1:10

JUNE 3

REFLECTION. St. Charles Lwanga and his companions were being forced to do things which they knew were immoral, and they refused to cooperate. They paid the price for this virtuous act with martyrdom.

There is always a price to pay when we refuse to cooperate with those who want us to do things which are contrary to our moral values.

PRAYER. *St. Charles Lwanga and his companions, pray for us.*

LL go to the same place; all were made from the dust, and to the dust all will return. —Eccl 3:20

JUNE 4

REFLECTION. At the beginning of Lent, on Ash Wednesday, we were reminded that we came from dust and unto dust we shall return.

It is good to remind ourselves of this truth every so often. We will not live forever. What are we doing in our lives that has eternal value?

PRAYER. *May Your Holy Spirit be breathed into the dust that I am.*

VERY day is wretched for those who are sorrowing, but to one who is cheerful, every day is a perpetual feast. **JUNE 5**

—Prov 15:15

REFLECTION. This proverb can be read as a simple statement of the truth, or it could be read as a challenge to make things better.

Can I share my joys with those around me so that they can experience the goodness of life? Can I share the heaviness of grief with those who are sorrowing?

PRAYER. *May I laugh with those who laugh and weep with those who weep.*

EFLECT on the decrees of the Lord and constantly meditate on his commandments. —Sir 6:37 **JUNE 6**

REFLECTION. If we regularly meditate on what God wants of us, then it will be easier to carry out God's Will.

If we spend all our time doing things of lesser value, watching frivilous TV programs, gossiping, eating or drinking too much, etc., then it will be more difficult to walk in God's ways.

PRAYER. *Guide me along Your paths, O Lord.*

NEVER discuss your plans with a fool, since he is unable to keep a confidence. —Sir 8:17

JUNE 7

REFLECTION. We should try to trust everyone, but we should trust them as much as they are trustworthy.

It is unfair to ask someone who is not capable of profound trust to keep a secret or to be discreet. That person does not have the ability to do what we would have asked of him or her.

PRAYER. *May I respect the gifts and limitations of those around me.*

A WHOLESOME tongue is a tree of life, but an undisciplined tongue crushes the spirit. —Prov 15:4

JUNE 8

REFLECTION. Someone whose speech is positive and edifying can build up the spirits of individuals and communities. Someone who is always negative or crude can tear those same people down.

We have an obligation to use our gift of speech to build up the Kingdom of God in our midst.

PRAYER. *O Lord, open my lips, and I shall praise Your Name.*

E WHO spares the rod hates his son, but one who loves his son will take care to discipline him. —Prov 13:24

JUNE 9

REFLECTION. While the idea of using physical violence against a child is abhorrent, there is still a truth in this proverb.

We have to be willing to correct our children when they do something wrong. Otherwise, the child will grow up without proper boundaries and possibly become self-centered and arrogant.

PRAYER. *Lord, teach me the way to properly guide my children and grandchildren.*

E GENEROUS in your gifts to the poor so that your blessing may be complete. —Sir 7:32

JUNE 10

REFLECTION. We think of helping the poor as a holy obligation, but it is more.

Giving to the poor is also a privilege, for when we help another, we are living in God's generosity that God showed us. We are truly showing ourselves to be in the image and likeness of God.

PRAYER. *Teach me to give more and more of myself, Lord, so that my life might reflect Your Goodness.*

NTRUST everything that you do to the Lord, and your plans will turn out to be successful. —Prov 16:3

JUNE 11

REFLECTION. St. Barnabas was an early Christian missionary and a sometimes companion of St. Paul.

Setting off on a missionary journey must have been exciting and frightening. One never knew what one would encounter. Likewise, in our Christian witness, we have to be willing to take risks in order to share the Good News in word and deed.

PRAYER. *St. Barnabas, pray for us.*

NYONE who winks with the eye causes trouble, but the one who rebukes promotes peace. —Prov 10:10

JUNE 12

REFLECTION. Going along with something that we know to be wrong (winking with one's eye) will not guarantee peace.

Rather, living an authentic life of integrity, even if that means that we have to say some things that others would prefer not to hear, is the only way to create a truly peaceful environment.

PRAYER. *Let me know, Lord, when I should let things go and when I should intervene.*

WISE man advances himself by his words; a prudent man is pleasing to the great. —Sir 20:27

JUNE 13

REFLECTION. St. Anthony of Padua was able to preach to the simplest people and to the leaders of great cities.

He made the Word of God the object of his study and the foundation of his life. This is why his statues often show him holding a book of the Gospels.

PRAYER. *May Your Word find a home in my thoughts and my heart.*

EVER fall into the trap of repeating a sin, for not even for one will you go unpunished. —Sir 7:8

JUNE 14

REFLECTION. It is one thing to make a mistake, and it is quite another to fall into a pattern of doing the same wrong thing over and over again.

Satan is the one who wants us to give up our efforts when we fall. We have to have the courage to stand up and start over again in God's grace.

PRAYER. *Jesus, You rose up three times on Your way to the Cross. Help me to rise again.*

A GOOD name is better than precious ointment, and the day of death than the day of birth. —Eccl 7:1

JUNE 15

REFLECTION. It is a good thing to have a good reputation. We feel proud of our efforts and others respect us.

Yet, we never know how things will turn out until the end arrives. Thus, we have to be cautious to be consistent in our commitment to live in God's grace every day of our lives.

PRAYER. *Grant me fidelity and consistency in my commitment to You, O Lord.*

THOSE with perverse hearts are abhorrent to the Lord, but those whose ways are blameless are dear to him. —Prov 11:20

JUNE 16

REFLECTION. God loves everyone, but those who do evil have turned their backs on God's love.

It is not that God has stopped loving them. They are incapable of experiencing that love because of their attitude and actions. To return to that love, they only have to turn their ways around again.

PRAYER. *Lord, I have turned my back on Your love. Help me to return to You.*

ISTEN eagerly to every godly conversation; allow no expression of wisdom to escape you. —Sir 6:35

JUNE 17

Reflection. It is good to hear good things. It raises our spirits and helps us to live as we should.

This is true of conversations, but it is also true of listening to good music, reading a good book, seeing a good movie, etc. The more we fill our lives with good things, the easier it is to be good.

Prayer. *May that which I say and hear and see be filled with Your goodness, Lord.*

ISDOM was beside him as a master craftsman, and I was his delight day after day. —Prov 8:30

JUNE 18

Reflection. On the day of creation, God used Wisdom as His guide on how to create and order all that exists.

This means that if we look around at the wonders of creation, we can discern the Wisdom of God being communicated to us through the beauty that God has created.

Prayer. *Be You praised, my Lord, for the beauty of all of creation.*

HOSE who are lazy become destitute, but those who are diligent gain wealth. —Prov 11:16b

JUNE 19

REFLECTION. We should not blame others for our difficulties or our shortcomings.

We are called to do the best we can with the talents and graces that God has given us. This doesn't mean that we will succeed all the time, but we have a much better chance at doing well if we truly commit ourselves.

PRAYER. *Awaken my spirit, O Lord, so that I might approach my tasks with enthusiasm.*

PRUDENT person does not flaunt his knowledge, but the heart of fools proclaims their folly. —Prov 12:23

JUNE 20

REFLECTION. We should not really have to brag about our abilities or accomplishments. It is better if we let them speak for themselves.

Foolish people are always calling attention to what they have done. It is sad when a person measures his self-worth by externals which are not all that important.

PRAYER. *May all I do, Lord, be for Your glory.*

HERE is nothing better for a man than to eat and drink and to experience pleasure in his achievements. —Eccl 2:24

JUNE 21

REFLECTION. It is often the simple things in life which bring the greatest pleasures. When we overplan events, they often turn out to be less than we would have hoped them to be.

When we settle for simple things, we are often surprised how they turn out to be so much more successful than we would have ever hoped.

PRAYER. *Tis a gift to be simple, tis a gift to be free.*

HE Lord will be your assurance and will keep your feet from the trap. —Prov 3:26

JUNE 22

REFLECTION. Saints John Fisher and Thomas More were executed by King Henry VIII because they refused to sign a document which said things which they knew were wrong.

They did not want to die, but when the time came for them to give that witness, they were ready to live and die for the truth as they knew it.

PRAYER. *Lord, may my commitment to You be more than a question of words and theories.*

EFUSE to ever tell a lie, for it is a habit that never has a positive result. —Sir 7:13

JUNE 23

REFLECTION. Telling the truth all the time can get you into trouble, but people will respect you for it.

Trying to get out of a messy situation with half-truths or evasive speech will not turn out well. It might give momentary relief to the difficulty, but it will leave one's spirit dirtied by one's failure to be transparent.

PRAYER. *May the truth always be on my lips, O God.*

ITHOUT prophecy the people become uncontrollable, but blessed are those who keep the law. —Prov 29:18

JUNE 24

REFLECTION. St. John the Baptist was the last prophet of the Old Testament and the first prophet of the New Testament. He prophesied in his mother's womb about the arrival of Jesus in the world.

We are all called to be prophets, speaking the Word of God, in our own times and in our own way.

PRAYER. *St. John the Baptist, pray for us.*

AN a man kindle a fire in his bosom without burning his clothes?

—Prov 6:27

JUNE 25

REFLECTION. If we let ourselves get enraged, it will not turn out well. If we become enflamed with lust, things will end poorly.

Emotions and feelings are not wrong or sinful, but we must use them in a Christian way lest we allow them to control our lives and we become prisoners to what we feel at that moment.

PRAYER. Lord, may I transform my desires and feelings so that they might serve the Kingdom.

SCOUNDREL, a villainous man, is he who specializes in crooked talk.

—Prov 6:12

JUNE 26

REFLECTION. The proverbs considered speech to be incredibly important for it was the main way that we communicate what we think and feel to others.

If speech is filled with dishonesty and vulgarity, we cannot expect the person uttering it to be a person of good character. Jesus said we will know them by the fruit they bear.

PRAYER. *Let every word that comes from my lips be pure and praiseworthy, my Lord.*

E QUICK to listen but deliberate in offering your answer. —Sir 5:11

JUNE 27

REFLECTION. We should always be willing to listen to what others say, but it is good to take time to ponder upon it before we commit ourselves to a course of action.

The Spirit of God tends to speak to us in whispers, so we must find time and quiet to discern the Spirit's promptings.

PRAYER. *Spirit of God, whisper Your Truths into the silence of my heart.*

ISDOM has built her house; she has hewn her seven pillars. —Prov 9:1

JUNE 28

REFLECTION. Wisdom has created a dwelling place for herself, and it is in the depths of our hearts.

Jesus breathed the Holy Spirit into the hearts of His disciples so that they might hear the voice of God within themselves and not have to search for God elsewhere. We have become temples of Wisdom, of the Holy Spirt.

PRAYER. *Come dwell in me, Spirit of God, and reveal Your Wisdom to me.*

HEN the righteous are in authority, the people rejoice. —Prov 29:2a

JUNE 29

REFLECTION. Saints Peter and Paul were called by God to lead the early Church.

They both agreed that their mission was one of love and service. Jesus even asked Peter if he loved Him three times, and when he said that he did, Jesus told him to shepherd His flock.

PRAYER. *Saints Peter and Paul, pray for us.*

WISE man is mightier than a strong man. —Prov 24:5a

JUNE 30

REFLECTION. The first martyrs of the Church were not powerful, but they were filled with the Wisdom of God for they allowed the Spirit to speak through them.

In the Scriptures we hear that they will kill us, but they will never be able to harm us for God will be at our side, even as we hang upon the cross.

PRAYER. *Holy Martyrs of the Church, guide me in my witness to the truth.*

DO YOUR work in the appointed time, and in his own time God will give you your reward. —Sir 51:30

JULY 1

REFLECTION. Our work, at its best, should not be considered an imposition or a curse. Rather, it can and should be seen as our way of continuing God's work of creation in this world.

Flipping a burger or doing the laundry can become a type of prayer if we do it with love. Everything depends upon our motivation.

PRAYER. *May all that I do today be in Your Name and in Your Love.*

THE fields of the poor may yield much food, but it is stolen from them through injustice. —Prov 13:23

JULY 2

REFLECTION. There is still terrible social injustice in the world and even in our own country. This is true even in countries which call themselves Christian.

It is important to examine the way our society works to make sure that we truly live a life of Christian values, especially in regard to how we treat the poor.

PRAYER. *May I never knowingly or unknowingly disrespect the poor and powerless.*

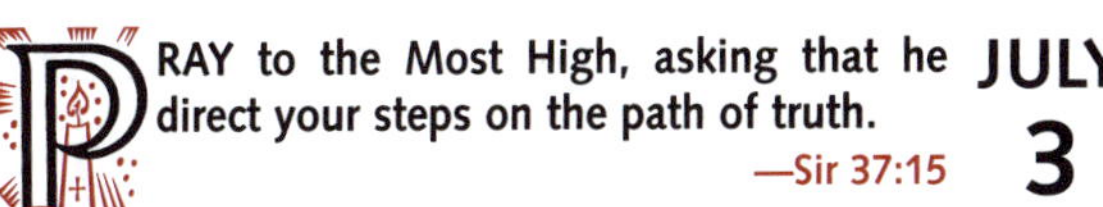

PRAY to the Most High, asking that he direct your steps on the path of truth. —Sir 37:15

JULY 3

REFLECTION. Arriving at the truth is not always easy. Like St. Thomas, we sometimes have to overcome a time of doubt to find the truth.

Doubting is not necessarily without a purpose in the spiritual life. St. Thomas, after doubting, realized that Jesus was his Lord and his God, a profession of faith more profound than that made by the other apostles.

PRAYER. *Lord Jesus, You are my Way, my Truth, and my Life.*

NO ONE who gives to the poor will suffer want. —Prov 28:27a

JULY 4

REFLECTION. Our country has been incredibly blessed by the providence of God and the work of our ancestors.

The proper way to respond to great blessing is to share it with those who most need it. Today might be a good day to reflect on what things and values we could share with our own citizens and those of other countries.

PRAYER. *God, may You continue to bless our nation and guide it in Your ways.*

O NOT rely on your wealth or say, "Now I am self-sufficient." —Sir 5:1

JULY 5

REFLECTION. It is always a temptation to think that our success is due totally to our own efforts. We can forget that God gave us the ability to do what we do, and the blessing for it to succeed.

Reminding ourselves of this every day can keep us from the danger of being arrogant or overly confident.

PRAYER. *Lord, all I am, all I do, is due to You.*

HEN you make a vow to God, do not delay in fulfilling it. —Eccl 5:3

JULY 6

REFLECTION. To be a person of integrity, we have to keep the promises that we make. This includes the promises that we make to God.

We should be careful as to what we promise God, especially in times of crisis; but once we make the resolution, we should be certain to keep it.

PRAYER. *Lord, make me firm in my commitments to You and to others.*

STUBBORN person will come to a bad end, and the one who loves danger will perish in it. —Sir 3:26

JULY 7

REFLECTION. There is a middle ground between being stubborn and foolhardy. Prudence is knowing when I should be willing to bend with the wind.

This doesn't mean that we don't stick to what we know is right or that we don't take risks because we believe that we are called to do so.

PRAYER. *May I always make decisions that are based upon prudence.*

AST your bread upon the waters, and eventually you will get it back. —Eccl 11:1

JULY 8

REFLECTION. When we do good things for others, we should not expect them to return the favor. The highest level of charity is doing good for others, even strangers, and expecting nothing in return.

This is why Jesus told His followers to invite people to our celebrations who could never invite us back.

PRAYER. *May my charity always be based on true love and not self-interest.*

HERE is a shame that leads to sin, and a shame that is honorable and gracious.
—Sir 4:21

JULY 9

REFLECTION. Guilt can be a good thing for it lets us know that we have done something wrong from which we should repent and ask forgiveness from God and from those whom we have hurt.

Shame is when we feel that we could never do anything right, and that God could never forgive us because we are unlovable.

PRAYER. *God, let me know when I have done wrong, but also that You always love me.*

Y CHILD, look after your father when he is old; do nothing to cause him grief as long as he lives. —Sir 3:12

JULY 10

REFLECTION. We tend to think of the obligations that parents have toward their children.

But there are also obligations that grown children have toward their parents. They might need help with medical care or daily chores or financial needs. Most of all they need our time and attention, our willingness to waste time with them.

PRAYER. *Thank You, God, for my parents. May You bless them now and in Your Kingdom.*

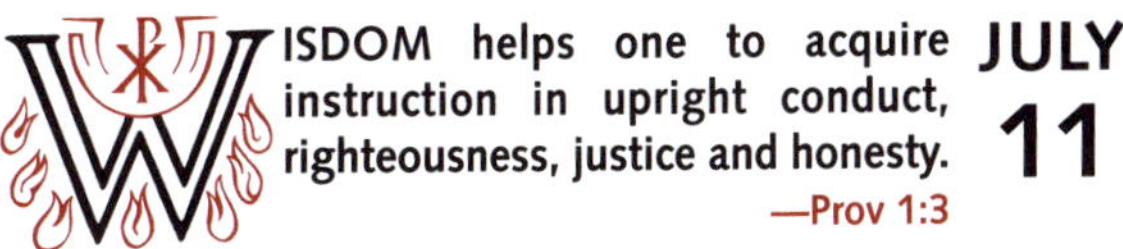

WISDOM helps one to acquire instruction in upright conduct, righteousness, justice and honesty. —Prov 1:3

JULY 11

REFLECTION. It takes a lifetime to learn the spiritual lessons that we need and to put them into practice. We are all "works in progress."

That is not a bad thing, for it reminds us that we always need the help of the Lord to make progress on our journey of faith.

PRAYER. *Never let me weary, Lord, of seeking to make myself more consistent with Your call.*

DO NOT envy a violent man or choose to emulate any of his ways. —Prov 3:31

JULY 12

REFLECTION. It might seem as if violent or arrogant people are the victors of messy situations in which they find themselves. This is an illusion.

When we choose violence of any sort, we are pushing others away and making ourselves lonelier and more isolated. Like Jesus, we have to choose to love even when we are on our way to the cross.

PRAYER. *May I always destroy the power of hate with my love.*

ONTEMPLATE the ant, you sluggard; observe its ways and gain wisdom.

—Prov 6:6

JULY 13

REFLECTION. The ant was considered to be one of the most industrious animals. It is always moving about to construct its nest and find food for the colony.

This proverb is encouraging us to put that much energy into our quest for wisdom. That is our true home, and that is what will nourish the deepest hunger of our hearts.

PRAYER. *May my greatest quest in life be to live in Your Wisdom.*

HE prayer of the lowly pierces the clouds; it does not rest until it reaches its goal.

—Sir 35:21

JULY 14

REFLECTION. God loves all of us, but God shows His love for us in different ways. When a person who is in true need raises a prayer up to the Lord, then God will certainly respond to that person.

This is true even when the difficulties from which the person is suffering are the person's own fault.

PRAYER. *Rend the heavens, O Lord, and come to my aid.*

ISDOM was created before all other things, and prudent understanding has existed from eternity. —Sir 1:4

JULY 15

REFLECTION. St. Bonaventure was a medieval theologian who spoke of the way that leads to God. He taught that we have to use the gifts God has given us (our senses, our intellect, our conscience, etc.) to find union with the All High.

His exemplar for one who succeeded in this quest was St. Francis of Assisi.

PRAYER. *Saints Bonaventure and Francis, pray for us.*

HERE many words are spoken, sin is not absent, but whoever restrains his tongue is prudent.
—Prov 10:19

JULY 16

REFLECTION. It is easy to get carried away with what we say. Following the flow of conversation, we end up saying things that we shouldn't because they are cruel or even untrue.

Saying less and correcting misimpressions that we hear from others can be both virtuous and prudent.

PRAYER. *Guard my tongue, Lord, so that what I say might be good and edifying.*

ICHES will be of no avail on the day of wrath, but righteousness delivers from death. —Prov 11:4

JULY 17

REFLECTION. We will not live forever, and on the final day we will be judged not by how much we have, but by how righteous and compassionate we have been.

Jesus distinguished between the riches of this world and spiritual riches. He always encouraged His listeners to store up treasure for life eternal.

PRAYER. *Guide me in my judgment of what the true treasure of my life is.*

OES Wisdom not call? Does Understanding not lift up her voice? —Prov 8:1

JULY 18

REFLECTION. At times it seems as if God is almost desperate for us to choose the path of wisdom and understanding. God did not create us to have a good time, but rather to learn to be as generous and loving as God is.

When we choose that path, we find that our lives become meaningful and fulfilled.

PRAYER. *Grant me wisdom and understanding, Lord, and let me live in their riches.*

O NOT be so confident of pardon that you add sin upon sin. —Sir 5:5

JULY 19

REFLECTION. While God is always willing to forgive us our sins, we should not be presumptuous, doing whatever we want and feeling that God has to forgive us.

Our relationship with God is not a game in which we try to get as much out of God as we can. It is a call to love and generosity.

PRAYER. *Help me turn from my sin, O Lord, for alone I cannot hope to succeed.*

SIMPLE person believes everything he hears, but a prudent person carefully considers every step. —Prov 14:15

JULY 20

REFLECTION. We are called to be trusting, but this does not mean that we should not be prudent. It is good to evaluate and even investigate what we hear and see, especially in this time of an overflow of information in the media.

A good rule of thumb is whether this so-called truth is consistent with the Gospels.

PRAYER. *Guide me in Truth, my Lord, and give me the grace of discernment.*

HOUGHTLESS words wound like a sword thrust, but the tongue of the wise produces healing. —Prov 12:18

JULY 21

REFLECTION. What we say to another can either wound or heal. It depends on what is in our heart.

This is why it is good to pause and pray over what we would like to say to that person. Thoughtlessly saying the first thing that comes to mind can be terribly destructive, and it is impossible to take those words back.

PRAYER. *Purify my lips, O Lord, so that all I say might be for the good of others.*

HE good woman is clothed with strength and dignity, and she can afford to laugh at the days to come. —Prov 31:25

JULY 22

REFLECTION. St. Mary Magdalene was called the proto apostle in ancient times for she was the first one to announce the resurrection of Jesus to the apostles.

Like Magdalene on Easter morning, may I search for the Risen Lord and rejoice when I hear Him call me by my name.

PRAYER. *St. Mary Magdalene, pray for me.*

O NOT become involved in too many matters; if you attempt too much, you will suffer the consequences.

—Sir 11:10

JULY 23

REFLECTION. Our lifestyle today can lead us to multi-tasking, trying to do many things at once. In a certain sense, that is admirable, but it can also get us into trouble.

Every so often we should take stock and ask ourselves whether we are trying to do too much. Do we have time to stop and smell the roses?

PRAYER. *Slow me down, O Lord, so that I might spend some time with You.*

AKE my words to heart, and the years of your life will be multiplied.

—Prov 4:10

JULY 24

REFLECTION. We do not know how long we will live. In Biblical times, they thought that if one were a God-fearing person, then that person would have a good and prosperous life.

There is no guarantee of this, but if we walk with the Lord, no matter how long we live, it will be a life filled with God's joy.

PRAYER. *Walk with me, Lord, and let me share my life with You.*

NYONE who refuses mercy to his peers cannot rightfully seek pardon for his own sins. —Sir 28:4

JULY 25

REFLECTION. In the Our Father we ask God to forgive us our trespasses as we forgive others.

If our hearts are open to forgive our neighbor, then they will also be open to receive the forgiveness that God is always offering us. If we have closed our hearts to forgiveness, then they will be closed to receive God's forgiveness as well.

PRAYER. *Forgive us our sins, as we forgive those who sin against us.*

O NOT reject the opinions of the aged, for they themselves were taught by their parents. —Sir 8:9

JULY 26

REFLECTION. Today we celebrate the feast day of the grandparents of Jesus. Our elderly relatives can be a source of wisdom that is passed down through the generations.

This means that we have to be willing to listen to what our elders say and to learn from their experiences in life.

PRAYER. *Saints Joachim and Anne, pray for us.*

E WHO oppresses the poor insults their Creator, but the one who is kind to the needy does him honor. —Prov 14:31

JULY 27

REFLECTION. It has often been asked why, if God is so good and loving, He permits people to be poor in the world.

We don't really have an answer for this question, but it does give us the opportunity to take the responsibility of caring for the poor into our own hands.

PRAYER. *Lord, may I assist You in Your acts of providence toward the needy.*

HE eyes of the Lord are everywhere, keeping a close watch on the evil and the good. —Prov 15:3

JULY 28

REFLECTION. When we say that God is watching us, it does not mean that God wants to catch us in some sin and then punish us.

Rather, like any loving parent, God wants to watch out for us, helping us to choose that which is good and helpful and to avoid that which is evil and would harm us.

PRAYER. *Keep watch over my life, O Lord, so that I might always walk in Your ways.*

CHOOSE honorable people for your dinner companions, and let your glory be in the fear of God. —Sir 9:16

JULY 29

REFLECTION. Saints Martha, Mary, and Lazarus showed Jesus hospitality by inviting Him and His disciples to stay with them during the feast days in Jerusalem.

Sharing a meal with another makes that person a companion (which literally means a person with whom one shares bread). It makes that companion a part of one's life.

PRAYER. *Bless the food I eat today and bless those with whom I share my meals.*

DO NOT answer without first listening, and do not interrupt while someone else is speaking. —Sir 11:8

JULY 30

REFLECTION. There is always the temptation to want to blurt out our opinion in a discussion, especially if we feel that we are right.

Yet, there is value in listening so that we recognize that we don't have a monopoly on the truth, and that the truth can be expressed in many different ways.

PRAYER. *Lord, teach me when to listen and when to speak.*

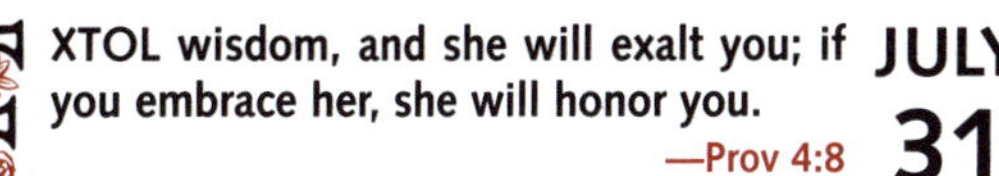

XTOL wisdom, and she will exalt you; if you embrace her, she will honor you.

—Prov 4:8

JULY 31

REFLECTION. Choosing God's wisdom means that we decide to see things through the eyes of God. This requires quite a bit of spiritual work.

We must root out those things which hinder our vision (selfishness, brokenness, etc.) and pray and study and reflect upon the truths that Jesus revealed to us.

PRAYER. *Lord, grant me wisdom, the attendant at Your throne.*

ET your eyes look straight ahead; fix your gaze on what lies before you.

—Prov 4:25

AUG. 1

REFLECTION. It is easy to become distracted by the difficulties of the world and our own personal difficulties. We can feel helpless in how we should respond to them.

Often the best thing we can do is to do what is possible and then place the rest of the mess in the hands of God.

PRAYER. *Let me address that which I can, Lord, and leave the rest to You.*

DO NOT abandon an old friend, for a new one will not adequately replace him. —Sir 9:10

AUG. 2

REFLECTION. Friends are not interchangeable, as if one person can replace another in our hearts.

Do I treat every person who comes into my life as a precious treasure that has been entrusted to me by a loving God, or do I at times use them and then discard them when they are no longer useful to me?

PRAYER. *Thank You for my friends, O Lord, and may You bless them abundantly for their goodness to me.*

GOOD fortune and bad, life and death, poverty, and wealth—all come from the Lord. —Sir 11:14

AUG. 3

REFLECTION. At times we would like to think that God only sends good things into our lives.

The Bible authors wrestled with the idea that God is in charge of everything. The good things that happen to us and even the bad things do not happen without God's knowledge.

PRAYER. *Lord, some things are beyond my understanding. Help me to trust.*

O NOT let kindness and fidelity leave you: fasten them around your neck and inscribe them on the tablet of your heart. —Prov 3:3

AUG. 4

REFLECTION. Kindness and fidelity are both a gift (something with which we are born) and a choice (something which we must develop and exercise).

These are two adjectives that are often used for God in the Hebrew Bible. This means that when we are kind and faithful, we are being God-like.

PRAYER. *May I be given the ability and commit myself to the practice of being kind and faithful.*

O NOT make up lies about your brother, or do the same to a friend. —Sir 7:12

AUG. 5

REFLECTION. While very few of us tell blatant lies about those around us, we are occasionally willing to tell half-truths or to exaggerate this or that.

We owe it to the person we are talking about and to the person to whom we are talking to be honest, lest what we say create rifts in our mutual relationships.

PRAYER. *Let me be a person of sincerity and integrity, Lord.*

HO has ever gone up to heaven and come down again? —Prov 30:4a

AUG. 6

REFLECTION. When Jesus was transfigured in glory, He was accompanied by Moses and Elijah to show that He was the fulfillment of the law and the prophets.

His glorious appearance also showed that the barriers between heaven and earth were disappearing and that the Kingdom of God was already dawning in our midst.

PRAYER. *Holy, holy, holy, is the Lord God Almighty. Heaven and Earth are filled with Your glory.*

O NOT engage in a dispute with an argumentative person and thereby heap wood upon his fire. —Sir 8:3

AUG. 7

REFLECTION. There are certain people with whom one cannot reason. They easily become angry and spew hateful words that are meant to hurt.

It is usually better to avoid that type of person, or if we cannot, to keep silent so that we do not stoke the furnace of that person's wrath.

PRAYER. *Lord, please heal the anger of _____. Bring Your peace into his/her heart.*

UT your feet into wisdom's fetters, and your neck into her collar. —Sir 6:24

AUG. 8

REFLECTION. St. Paul says that we can be prisoners of sin or prisoners of the love of the Lord. We have to belong to one or the other.

Likewise, we can be bound to foolishness and selfishness, or we can be bound to wisdom and understanding. The latter brings us to true freedom.

PRAYER. *Shower Your wisdom upon my mind and my heart so that I might live in Your light.*

HE Lord reserves his wisdom for the upright and is a shield to those who lead blameless lives. —Prov 2:7

AUG. 9

REFLECTION. St. Teresa Benedicta of the Cross, Edith Stein, was a great philosopher and a faithful Carmelite nun. She died in a concentration camp.

God's promise to be our shield does not mean that all will be peaceful and successful in our lives, but rather that we will have the opportunity to love without limit.

PRAYER. *St. Teresa Benedicta of the Cross, pray for us.*

OVE and the performance of good works are the gift of the Lord. —Sir 11:15

AUG. 10

REFLECTION. St. Lawrence was a deacon of the Church of Rome who willingly gave up his life as a martyr.

He was known to be someone who truly became a person filled with love in the way that he treated the poor of the Church of Rome and for the way he was willing to die for the faith.

PRAYER. *St. Lawrence, deacon and martyr, pray for us.*

LESSED is the one who listens to me, who keeps watch daily at my gates. —Prov 8:33

AUG. 11

REFLECTION. St. Clare is said to have been clear (the meaning of the name Clare) in name and in life. She was transparent in her love of Christ.

Would that, if people could see the innermost secrets of our hearts, they would be edified with how consistent what we say and do is with what we hold in our hearts.

PRAYER. *St. Clare of Assisi, pray for us.*

FAITHFUL friend is a sure shelter; anyone who finds one possesses a treasure.
—Sir 6:14

AUG. 12

REFLECTION. We often think in terms of having a friend who will back us up when we truly need that person's presence and assistance.

It might be helpful to ask ourselves today if we have been true friends to those around us. Are we generous toward them with time and talent?

PRAYER. *May I always be a good friend to those whom I like, and especially to those who need my friendship.*

ILIGENT labor always yields profit, but idle conversation only leads to poverty.
—Prov 14:23

AUG. 13

REFLECTION. We say that words are cheap. It is easy to talk about what we could or should do, but it is only when we put our intentions into action that they become real and effective.

This is why St. James said that if our faith is only words, it is only a theory. It is when we put it into action that it becomes alive and useful.

PRAYER. *May the words of my mouth be lived in my actions today.*

UST as he came forth naked from his mother's womb, so shall he depart, naked as he came. —Eccl 5:14

AUG. 14

REFLECTION. St. Maximilian Kolbe had a strong devotion to the Blessed Virgin Mary. He built a very large apostolate in her honor.

Yet, when the time came for him to be taken to prison by the Nazis, he did not despair. All that he had done was in honor of Mary, and now he was placing it back in her hands.

PRAYER. *St. Maximilian, teach us to trust in the protection of our Blessed Virgin Mary.*

LL the works of God are marvelous, and everything that he commands will occur at the designated time. —Sir 39:16

AUG. 15

REFLECTION. At the end of her life upon this earth, God extended a special honor to the Blessed Virgin Mary, taking her up into heaven body and soul.

That which happened to her foretells what will happen to each one of us at the end of time. Like her, God will call us home to be with Him forever.

PRAYER. *Mary, assumed into heaven body and soul, intercede for us to your Son.*

E WHO fears the Lord provides strong security, and in him one's children will find a refuge. —Prov 14:26

AUG. 16

REFLECTION. The fear of the Lord is not to be afraid of God, but rather to recognize God's greatness and glory.

If we live with that attitude, our children and grandchildren will see our example and hopefully will want to live in that same sense of peace and joy that we have found.

PRAYER. *God, I pray for the faith of everyone in my family, especially those who seem to be wavering.*

O NOT flaunt your righteousness before the Lord or assert your wisdom in the presence of the king. —Sir 7:5

AUG. 17

REFLECTION. When the Pharisee and the Publican went to the temple, the Pharisee bragged about his accomplishments while the Publican humbly asked for mercy.

If we think that we have done everything well and that God owes us, then we cannot open our hearts like the Publican to receive God's mercy.

PRAYER. *Have mercy on me, O God, for I have sinned.*

EFUSE to be provoked by an insolent man, for he may seek to trap you in your own words. —Sir 8:11

AUG. 18

REFLECTION. There are people with whom one cannot have an honest conversation. They often seem to be playing games when they talk with us.

We have to be careful not to give in to their ploys. We should try to be honest and sincere and at times silent when it isn't worth saying something.

PRAYER. *Lord, teach me when to speak and teach me when to hold my tongue.*

TRANQUIL heart gives life to the body, but envy causes the bones to rot. —Prov 14:30

AUG. 19

REFLECTION. If we spend too much time reflecting on how unfair life is and being jealous of others, we will only frustrate ourselves and we will miss out on the goodness with which God has blessed us.

We will only find peace if we can fill our life with a sense of gratitude and surrender to God's will for us.

PRAYER. *Thank You, God, for what You have made me and what You have given me.*

NE who speaks incessantly is feared in his city, and one who is rash in his speech is despised. —Sir 9:18

AUG. 20

REFLECTION. The fact that speech is a gift from God does not mean that we should use it incessantly or carelessly.

We should be careful how much we talk, lest we be seen as someone who only wants to monopolize a conversation. We should be careful about what we say, lest we say things that are foolish and even hurtful.

PRAYER. *May every word of my mouth be filled with Your wisdom and prudence.*

HE netherworld and the abyss lie open to the Lord; how much more is this true of the human heart. —Prov 15:11

AUG. 21

REFLECTION. The ancients believed that the netherworld (the afterlife) was far beyond our comprehension. It is a place of mystery, and yet God knows it intimately.

In the same sense, our own hearts can seem to be complex and confusing, and yet God knows them well. God knows us better than we know ourselves.

PRAYER. *Plumb the depths of my heart, O Lord, and reveal to me its mysteries.*

O NOT ask the Lord for a position of authority or the king for a seat of honor. —Sir 7:4

AUG. 22

REFLECTION. Today we celebrate the feast of the Queenship of the Blessed Virgin Mary. She is the queen of heaven and earth.

This should not be interpreted in terms of power and glory, but rather in terms of love and care. There is no one for whom she does not intercede with her loving Son.

PRAYER. *Mary, Queen of heaven and earth, pray for us.*

OMETIMES a path may seem to be right, but in the end it leads to death. —Prov 16:25

AUG. 23

REFLECTION. We have to be willing to reevaluate our course of action every so often. What we choose one day might very well prove to be a mistake in the long run.

This is not a disaster, as long as we are humble enough to admit that we made a mistake and are pliable enough to change our course of action.

PRAYER. *Jesus, You are the way, the truth, and the life. Guide me in Your ways.*

N HONORABLE name is more to be desired than great riches, and high esteem is preferable to silver and gold.
—Prov 22:1

AUG. 24

REFLECTION. St. Bartholomew, also known as Nathaniel, was honored by Jesus who called him a true Israelite. Unlike many of those around him, he sought true wisdom while he reflected upon Holy Scripture under the fig tree.

May we, like him, one day see the angels ascending to and descending from heaven.

PRAYER. *St. Bartholomew, teach us to be like you, true seekers of the eternal truth.*

HE Lord tears down the proud man's house, but he preserves the widow's boundaries. —Prov 15:25

AUG. 25

REFLECTION. The Lord shows a special preference toward those who need Him most. They are the ones who are most willing to admit their dependance upon His providence.

Those who are rich and self-sufficient have made themselves into their own gods, but those who are broken and needy reach out to God with hope and yearning.

PRAYER. *God, may I recognize myself as someone who truly needs Your presence and Your providence.*

T IS better to be a patient person rather than a warrior. —Prov 16:32

AUG. 26

REFLECTION. Looking at someone who is patient, we might make the mistake of judging that person to be weak and fragile.

But it takes real courage and wisdom to be patient in times of difficulty. Patience is a sign that a person is not trying to be in charge, but rather leaves everything in the hands of God.

PRAYER. *May I not be afraid to be humble and patient throughout the course of my life.*

IVE heed, my son, to your father's instruction, do not reject your mother's teaching. —Prov 1:8

AUG. 27

REFLECTION. St. Monica constantly prayed for the conversion of her son, St. Augustine. She was thrilled when he turned from his confused ways and embraced the faith.

We have to remember the power of our prayers. They are acts of love raised up to the Lord so that His love and ours might visit the person for whom we are praying.

PRAYER. *St. Monica, please intercede for my loved ones, especially for those who seem to be lost.*

F YOU cry out for the gift of discernment and plead for understanding ... then you will understand the fear of the Lord and discover the knowledge of God. —Prov 2:3, 5

AUG. 28

REFLECTION. St. Augustine sought the truth, often in the wrong places. He finally looked into his own heart and found that for which he had always been striving.

We, like St. Augustine, must listen to the voice of the Spirit in our hearts telling us how much God has always loved us and desired us to live in that love.

PRAYER. *St. Augustine, guide me in my search for the fear and knowledge of God.*

E STEADFAST in your convictions and consistent in your speech. —Sir 5:10

AUG. 29

REFLECTION. St. John the Baptist was fearless in his preaching, even telling the king that his marriage to the divorced wife of his brother was against the law of Israel. For this, he was martyred.

He is an example to us to remind us to stand up for the truth, no matter what the cost might be.

PRAYER. *St. John the Baptist, teach me to be a faithful witness to the truth of God.*

ONE who forgives a misdeed fosters friendship, but he who divulges it separates good friends. —Prov 17:9

AUG. 30

REFLECTION. How should we react to a hurtful deed done to us? If we try to let it go, then it will not poison our heart and mind.

However, if we share the story with someone else to get that person on our side, it will only create more division and it will multiply the effects of the original hurt.

PRAYER. *God, may I heal the hurts of this world with my love.*

NOTHING is more evil than one who loves money, for such a person places his soul on sale. —Sir 10:8

AUG. 31

REFLECTION. We live in a consumeristic society which often bases the worth of a person on how much that person owns. We can buy into those values without even knowing it.

The alternative would be to simplify our lives. The more we give away and the less we have is a sign of how free we are from the wrong values.

PRAYER. *May I and my family have what we need, but not so much that we get lost in what we possess.*

HE crucible is for silver and the furnace is for gold, but it is the Lord who tests the heart. —Prov 17:3

SEPT. 1

REFLECTION. The crucible and furnace are used to burn off impurities from precious metals. It is the Lord who burns off the impurities of our hearts.

Our motives are always a bit mixed. We think we are doing something for the right reason, but deep down there is a bit of self-interest. God helps us to see this and overcome it.

PRAYER. *Purify my heart, O Lord, with the fire of Your love.*

O ONE pities a person who associates with sinners and becomes involved in their evil deeds. —Sir 12:14

SEPT. 2

REFLECTION. We were all warned to be careful of the company we keep. Yet sometimes we associate with people who drag us down by their example and, at times, by their invitation to be like them.

Jesus never avoided sinners, but He did have the courage to call them to change their ways.

PRAYER. *I pray for those in my life who have lost their way.*

HE greater you are, the greater should be your humility; in this way you will find favor with the Lord. —Sir 3:18

SEPT. 3

REFLECTION. Pope St. Gregory the Great desired to be a lowly one, but the Lord called him to lead the Church. It was his humility that truly made him great.

When we are given positions of responsibility (in the Church, the community, the family), we must use these roles as an opportunity for humble service of others.

PRAYER. *St. Gregory the Great, pray for me.*

T IS better to come upon a bear robbed of her cubs rather than confronting a fool in his folly. —Prov 17:12

SEPT. 4

REFLECTION. A bear that loses its cubs is bound to be very ferocious. This proverb reminds us that a person who does not live a life of wisdom is even more dangerous than that.

A fool in Wisdom Literature is selfish, arrogant, covetous, impetuous, etc. These flaws always lead to a tragic outcome.

PRAYER. *May wisdom be my protector and guide as I follow Your call.*

T IS not right to fine the innocent or to flog princes for their integrity. —Prov 17:26

SEPT. 5

REFLECTION. One of the most important responsibilities of those who have authority is to guarantee justice, especially for the poor and weak.

We should never allow the innocent to suffer unjustly, whether it be those immediately around us or those who live at the other end of the world, for they are all our sisters and our brothers.

PRAYER. *May I always defend those who suffer unjustly.*

ETURN to the Lord and renounce your wicked ways; pray in his presence and lessen your offense. —Sir 17:25

SEPT. 6

REFLECTION. We are all sinners; we are all broken. We should follow God's ways, yet when we sin, we should turn back to the Lord as soon as possible.

Conversion is not for tomorrow or for a distant time in the future. Today is the day of salvation; today is the day to turn back to the ways of the Lord.

PRAYER. *Lord, purify my heart and my ways so that I might walk again in Your path.*

O NOT say, "What do I need, and what further benefits can be mine?"

—Sir 11:23

SEPT. 7

REFLECTION. If we concentrate on those things which we do not have and which we would like to possess, then we will end up being frustrated and resentful.

If, on the other hand, we concentrate with a spirit of gratitude upon all the things we have received, then we will be filled with a sense of peace.

PRAYER. *Thank You, Lord, for all the ways that You have blessed my life.*

HE path of the righteous is like the light of dawn which increases in brightness to the fullness of day.

—Prov 4:18

SEPT. 8

REFLECTION. Mary was protected from sin and selfishness from the moment of her conception. We call that belief the dogma of the Immaculate Conception.

While we don't have that innocence, we can ask Mary to intercede for us so that we might be purified in God's love, forgiveness, and compassion.

PRAYER. *Mary, conceived without sin, pray for us who have recourse to you.*

FOOL steps boldly into a house, whereas the well-bred person waits outside respectfully. —Sir 21:22

SEPT. 9

REFLECTION. We are called to recognize certain boundaries in our lives and those of others which should be respected.

We don't have to know everything, or be part of everything, or be the center of attention. There is a time when we should be patient and "stand outside" until people invite us into their lives.

PRAYER. *May I always respect the space that others need.*

AN a fool purchase wisdom if he has no desire to learn? —Prov 17:16b

SEPT. 10

REFLECTION. True wisdom, true spiritual insight, requires effort. Granted, it is a gift from God, but it is a gift for which we must prepare our hearts.

This means cultivating a practice of prayer, spiritual reading, examination of conscience, and all the other spiritual disciplines which help us to welcome God's wisdom into our lives.

PRAYER. *Lord, give me the will to find You, and the willingness to work for that goal.*

A MAN'S attire and his hearty laughter, as well as the way he walks, reveal his character. —Sir 19:30

SEPT. 11

REFLECTION. It is good to remember that our external attributes reveal quite a bit about ourselves. Even before we say a word, people have a sense of who we are.

Without getting too obsessive about how we look, we should recognize that these things are not only our concerns, but also tell others what we think of them.

PRAYER. *Lord, may I always present myself in a way that is respectful to others.*

ONE who uses words sparingly is truly wise. —Prov 17:27a

SEPT. 12

REFLECTION. There is a time to speak and a time to be silent. Rather than trying to be the center of attention, we could try to truly listen to what others are saying.

God spoke to Elijah on the holy mountain in a small whispering voice. He did not use many words to communicate His revelation.

PRAYER. *Lord, may I meet You in the silence of my heart.*

ETWEEN morning and evening changes occur; all things are fleeting in the sight of the Lord. —Sir 18:26

SEPT. 13

REFLECTION. We live in a fast-paced world, and things are always changing. If we try to hold on to the past or try to make sure that things don't change in our lives in the future, we will only become frustrated.

Jesus said that the good steward is the one who can use both the old and the new.

PRAYER. *Lord, may I honor both the old and the new in my life.*

HE Lord is awe-inspiring in his majesty, and marvelous in his power. —Sir 43:29

SEPT. 14

REFLECTION. It is easy to look upon the Cross as humiliation. Yet, the Gospel of John considers it to be Jesus' hour of glory.

Glory is redefined in this Gospel as the outpouring of love. We most clearly see how much God loves us when we see His Son die on the Cross out of love for us.

PRAYER. *May I take up my cross each day as a sign of my love for You and those around me.*

DO NOT turn your back on those who weep, but mourn with those who mourn. —Sir 7:34

SEPT. 15

REFLECTION. The Blessed Virgin Mary shared in the sufferings of her only Son as He died on the Cross. She is an example to us of how we should practice a similar compassion.

We cannot always solve the problems of those around us, but we can always be one with them in their difficulties.

PRAYER. *Mary, Our Lady of Sorrows, show your compassion to me and those who are suffering.*

WHOEVER throws a stone straight up into the air will see it descend on his own head. —Sir 27:25

SEPT. 16

REFLECTION. We often don't realize that when we try to hurt others, we are the ones who suffer the most. We become caught up in our own plans.

We end up being nasty and bitter people who are lonelier for how we have pushed others out of our lives.

PRAYER. *May I never hurt others, but rather seek to heal them with my love.*

E CONTENT with what you have, whether much or little, and you will not be scorned as a guest. —Sir 29:23

SEPT. 17

Reflection. It is not always easy to accept what we have. We tend to speak in terms of "would have, could have, should have."

In second guessing our situation, we are questioning God's Will for us. When we surrender to that Will, we find a profound peace for we realize that this is where God wants us to be.

Prayer. *Lord, let me be satisfied with what Your providence has given me.*

HE conversation of the devout is always wise, but the fool is as changeable as the moon. —Sir 27:11

SEPT. 18

Reflection. When we say something, do we really mean it? Or is our speech simply a form of entertainment which wanders here and there based upon what our audience wants to hear.

It is not always easy to do it, but we should mean what we say and live what we mean.

Prayer. *May the words of my mouth reflect the wisdom of my heart.*

HOEVER is kind to the poor lends to the Lord who will recompense him for his kindness. —Prov 19:17

SEPT. 19

REFLECTION. In the Gospel of Luke, the poor are the Anawim, the chosen ones of the Lord. In the Gospel of Matthew, we hear in the parable of the sheep and the goats that we will be judged upon our compassion to the poor.

Jesus Himself was born and lived among the poor.

PRAYER. *May I see Your face, O Lord, in the faces of the poor.*

TRUE friend is one at all times, and a brother is born to render help in time of need. —Prov 17:17

SEPT. 20

REFLECTION. Friendship is not just a question of getting along with someone or finding that person's presence entertaining.

True friendship, like that of King David and Jonathan, is a commitment to be there for each other when one's presence and assistance is needed. This is why Jesus can call us His friends.

PRAYER. *Lord, teach me to be a true friend to the people You have placed into my life.*

IVE to the Most High as he has given to you, as generously as your means allow. —Sir 35:12

SEPT. 21

REFLECTION. The evangelist Matthew presents the story of Jesus as the fulfillment of all of the promises that God had made to Israel throughout its history.

God continues to fulfill those promises in our own personal history. Our only possible response to the generosity God has shown to us is a tremendous sense of gratitude.

PRAYER. *As You have loved me, O Lord, so may I also love You.*

NE with a violent temper must bear the consequences; if you spare him, you make his evil worse. —Prov 19:19

SEPT. 22

REFLECTION. While we are called to be patient and understanding with the flaws of others, we are also called to intervene when those flaws cause great pain to those around us.

Ignoring or going along with the abuse means that we condemn that person to the hell of being isolated and rejected.

PRAYER. *Lord, teach me when to be patient and when to intervene.*

LESSED is the man who guards himself against temptation. —Prov 28:14a

SEPT. 23

REFLECTION. We are called to be honest with ourselves about how weak we are and to try to avoid situations which could easily lead us into sin.

It is not that we want to reject the joys of this world, but we have to admit that some joys could lead us down the wrong path.

PRAYER. *Grant me the strength, O Lord to overcome temptation in my life.*

INE encourages recklessness and strong drink leads to brawls. —Prov 20:1

SEPT. 24

REFLECTION. We must be realistic as to how we react to strong drink. It often lowers our inhibitions, and we end up doing things that we normally would not do.

We should occasionally ask ourselves how much we really need that drink at the end of the day, and whether it is a good thing.

PRAYER. *God, may I be careful not to overindulge in things that are not good for me.*

THE fear of the Lord leads to life, enabling one to eat and sleep without fear of harm. —Prov 19:23

SEPT. 25

REFLECTION. When we truly trust in the Lord, we find a sense of peace for we recognize that God is in control of our lives.

It doesn't mean that bad things will never happen to us, but it does mean that we will recognize how God is present to us in good times and in bad.

PRAYER. *Lord, Your Kingdom come, Your Will be done, on earth as it is in heaven.*

DO NOT neglect to visit the sick, for as a result of such deeds you will be loved. —Sir 7:35

SEPT. 26

REFLECTION. This is the feast of Saints Cosmas and Damian, two brothers and doctors who died as martyrs for the faith.

It is not a bad thing to pray for the health care professionals who care for us. We should also reach out to those who are sick so that we might help them in their need.

PRAYER. *Saints Cosmas and Damian, help us to pray for the sick and those who care for them.*

O NOT withhold kindness from anyone to whom it is due. —Prov 3:27

SEPT. 27

REFLECTION. St. Vincent de Paul was famous for his kind and generous treatment of the poor. In fact, to this day many parishes have St. Vincent de Paul societies to continue that outreach.

What type of poor am I called to serve: those who are poor financially, spiritually, emotionally, etc.? What can I do to ease their difficulties?

PRAYER. *St. Vincent de Paul, teach me how to be generous to those in need.*

O NOT use your mouth for coarse and foul language since that involves sinful speech. —Sir 23:13

SEPT. 28

REFLECTION. Swearing and cussing are not something a Christian should do. These things do not build others up, but rather create further division.

If one were to pause and say a prayer for that person or situation which is annoying us, then one would be using words as God always intended them to be used.

PRAYER. *Lord, cleanse my mouth of every impurity.*

ETURN to the Most High, turn away from iniquity, and he will guide you out of darkness... —Sir 17:26

SEPT. 29

REFLECTION. The archangels serve God by communicating God's will to us. They fight evil (Michael), invite us to surrender to God's call (Gabriel), and heal us of our woundedness (Raphael).

We are not alone in our faith journey. We are always accompanied by these spiritual creatures who continue to reveal God's Will to us each day.

PRAYER. *Saints Michael, Gabriel and Raphael, pray for us.*

HE fount of wisdom is God's word in the highest heaven, and her ways are the eternal laws. —Sir 1:5

SEPT. 30

REFLECTION. St. Jerome, who translated the Bible into Latin, said that the person who does not know the Sacred Scriptures does not truly know God.

It is a good and holy thing to read a bit of Scripture each day and to meditate on how we might apply its lessons to our daily life.

PRAYER. *Word of God, speak to me. Guide me along the right path.*

HE upright will live in the land, and those who are innocent will remain there. —Prov 2:21

OCT. 1

REFLECTION. St. Thérèse of Lisieux said that very few of us are called to do extraordinary things. Still, we can do small things with extraordinary love.

This means that the everyday events of our lives should be consecrated in God's love. They can become visible signs of the grace and compassion of God in the world.

PRAYER. *St. Thérèse, teach us to love God and others in the small events of our lives.*

HOEVER listens to me will be secure and live in peace without fear of disaster. —Prov 1:33

OCT. 2

REFLECTION. God loves us so much that we have been assigned guardian angels, spiritual creatures who watch over us and guide us along the right path.

One of their most important responsibilities is to continuously remind us to live in a way that is consistent with what Jesus taught us.

PRAYER. *Guardian Angel, guide and protect me each day of my life.*

FALSE witness will perish, but a truthful witness will never be silenced.

—Prov 21:28

OCT. 3

REFLECTION. We are called to be witnesses to the truth. This might be difficult and even threatening at times.

St. John the Baptist is an example of someone who paid the price for proclaiming the truth. We must have the courage to give witness to that truth in everything that we say or do.

PRAYER. *Lord, guide me in the way of Your truth.*

OOK at the rainbow and praise its Maker, for it glows with a surpassing beauty.

—Sir 43:11

OCT. 4

REFLECTION. St. Francis of Assisi praised the God of all creation, especially in his Canticle of the Creatures. He saw nature as a revelation of God's goodness and generosity.

Today might be a good day to slow down and look around at the marvels of the birds and trees and the sun and the moon.

PRAYER. *St. Francis, teach us to be filled with wonder and awe at the world around us.*

HOSE who fear the Lord keep their heart prepared and humble themselves before him. —Sir 2:17

OCT. 5

REFLECTION. St. Faustina experienced the compassion of God and shared her insights in her promotion of devotion to Divine Mercy.

God is always merciful to us, but we must recognize our need for that mercy and open our hearts to it so that it might take root in our hearts.

PRAYER. *Loving, merciful God, may I experience Your compassion and the healing of Your love.*

HE rich and the poor have this in common: all of them were made by the Lord. —Prov 22:2

OCT. 6

REFLECTION. It is easy to think that one is superior to others if one is gifted or rich. Yet, God created all of us and loves every one of us.

We don't really know why some of us seem to be treated differently by God, but we can be sure that God loves us all as we are.

PRAYER. *God, may I always be grateful for what You have created me to be.*

HE teaching of the wise is a fountain of life enabling one to avoid the snares of death. —Prov 13:14

OCT. 7

REFLECTION. Our Blessed Lady, by her example of surrender to the will of God, taught us what true wisdom means: embracing and living what God had called us to be and to do.

The rosary is a means of reflecting upon her obedience and that of her Son to the will of the Father.

PRAYER. *Our Lady of the Rosary, pray for us now and at the hour of our death.*

UDGE your neighbor's feelings by your own, and be thoughtful in every respect. —Sir 31:15

OCT. 8

REFLECTION. It is easy to see the flaws of those around us and to blame them for all our difficulties.

Jesus taught us to view our neighbor as someone who needs and deserves our love and compassion. We are called to be a Good Samaritan to everyone whom we meet.

PRAYER. *Lord, teach me to be a good neighbor to everyone I encounter today.*

IKE one who clutches at shadows or chases the wind is someone who pays heed to dreams. —Sir 34:2

OCT. 9

REFLECTION. While God occasionally speaks to us through dreams, most of the time our dreams are expressions of our own hopes or anxieties.

We have to be careful in determining how God is speaking to us. This is why it is important to have a spiritual director or friend to help us find balance in our spiritual life.

PRAYER. *Loving God, please help me to understand what You want of me.*

NYONE who plans to do evil earns a reputation for intrigue. —Prov 24:8

OCT. 10

REFLECTION. Wisdom literature instructs us on how to live a good life, but it also warns us against choosing anything that is evil or selfish or arrogant.

People can see through the image we would like to present them concerning ourselves. They can sense what is truly in our hearts, whether it be good or evil.

PRAYER. *Lord, may I always be a person of transparency and integrity.*

KINDNESS in speech multiplies friends, and a gracious tongue leads to friendly responses. —Sir 6:5

OCT. 11

REFLECTION. Pope Saint John XXIII was well known for his example of kindness and welcome toward all those whom he met.

A kind word to a stranger or someone who is going through difficulty can make all of the difference in the world. We are called to use our gift of speech to build up and not to tear down.

PRAYER. *May the words of my mouth always be kind and compassionate.*

EAT what is set before you like a well-bred person; do not gulp down your food and make yourself objectionable. —Sir 31:16

OCT. 12

REFLECTION. Good manners might not seem to have much to do with our faith, but they are an expression of respect toward those with whom we are eating.

Jesus showed the importance of meals when He gave us the gift of His body and blood in the context of a meal, the Last Supper.

PRAYER. *Lord, may I always give an example of good manners in all that I do.*

NYONE who offers an honest answer gives a kiss on the lips. —Prov 24:26

OCT. 13

REFLECTION. There are times that we really do not want to hear the truth from others. We wish they would go along with our self-delusions.

The kindest thing that a person could do for us is to gently share the truth with us, a truth which we desperately need to hear.

PRAYER. *May I always respect those who have the love and courage to tell me the truth.*

F YOUR enemy is thirsty, offer him something to drink. —Prov 25:21b

OCT. 14

REFLECTION. One of the tendencies in life is to try to get back at those whom we think have hurt either us or someone we love.

Jesus always judged His enemies as being people who were wounded and what they were doing as a symptom of that brokenness. The last thing He wanted to do was to make their pain worse.

PRAYER. *Jesus, teach me to forgive others even as You forgave Your persecutors on the Cross.*

LESSED is the person who has found wisdom, the one who has gained understanding. —Prov 3:13

OCT. 15

REFLECTION. St. Teresa of Avila, a Doctor of the Church, discovered and shared the way to encounter our Lord in prayer and contemplation.

Each day we are called to set aside a little time to invite the Lord into our hearts. This is never a waste of time, but rather the most important thing we can do for ourselves and our world.

PRAYER. *St. Teresa, please intercede for me as I seek to know and love God better.*

AN'S compassion is for his neighbor, but the compassion of the Lord extends to everyone. —Sir 18:13

OCT. 16

REFLECTION. St. Margaret Mary Alacoque received revelations about the Sacred Heart of Jesus, a devotion which emphasized the overwhelming love God has for all of us.

There is no one who was ever created whom God did not love with all His heart. As we see through Jesus' death on the Cross, He loves us literally to death.

PRAYER. *Most Sacred Heart of Jesus, have mercy on us.*

E AWARE at all times of the condition of your flocks and take good care of your herds. —Prov 27:23

OCT. 17

REFLECTION. Even as he was being carried to his martyrdom in Rome, St. Ignatius of Antioch was profoundly concerned for the Christian communities to which he wrote a series of letters.

Whatever role of authority that God has given us (Church, family, work, friends) should be lived in service of those who have been placed in our care.

PRAYER. *Jesus, Good Shepherd, teach me how to care for Your flock.*

NDEAR yourself to the community and bow your head in the presence of authority. —Sir 4:7

OCT. 18

REFLECTION. St. Luke recognized the need for surrender to the authority of God in our lives (whether directly from God or through those whom God has placed in positions of authority).

Our obedience reflects the obedience of Jesus to the will of the Father in His incarnation and His death on the Cross.

PRAYER. *St. Luke, teach us to obey the will of God in our lives with great generosity of spirit.*

E SINCERE of heart and steadfast; and do not be alarmed when confronted with adversity. —Sir 2:2

OCT. 19

REFLECTION. When we face difficulties in our lives, it is not a sign that we are doing something wrong. It might, in fact, be a sign that we have been called to embrace our cross just as Jesus did.

Success in our Christian life is not based on how well things are going, but rather upon how much we are loving.

PRAYER. *Jesus, teach me to embrace my own cross just as You did Yours.*

T IS not good to eat too much honey, nor is it honorable to seek one's own honor. —Prov 25:27

OCT. 20

REFLECTION. We can get into trouble when we start doing or saying things to win the approval of others. We have to have the courage to do what is right, no matter what the consequences are.

In this, Jesus is our example of true humility. He did not seek His own honor, but rather that of the Father.

PRAYER. *Lord, may I always attribute the good that I do to Your grace and goodness.*

HE offering of the righteous enriches the altar, and its pleasing odor rises before the Most High. —Sir 35:8

OCT. 21

REFLECTION. Every good word that we say, every good deed that we do, every prayer that we utter can be thought of as a sacrifice of love offered to God.

Our liturgy is not something that is only offered within our church buildings, but is rather something that is present in everything good and holy that we do.

PRAYER. *Lord, consecrate all I do and say and pray in Your love.*

VERY friend can say, "I too am your friend," but some are friends in name only. —Sir 37:1

OCT. 22

REFLECTION. We need to test our friendships to make sure that they are not only relationships based upon convenience or entertainment or profit. True friendship should be much more.

One can measure the authenticity of a friendship by how it survives during times of difficulties and testing. Will your friend always be there for you?

PRAYER. *Lord, may I find true friends in my life and be a true friend to others.*

RUST your own judgment, for you have no counselor more reliable for you.

—Sir 37:13

OCT. 23

REFLECTION. We have to trust our own gut feelings and judgments. That, of course, is based upon the fact that we have worked to form a good conscience based upon Gospel values.

Ultimately, not every choice we make will be perfect. We are only called to do the best we can each day of our lives.

PRAYER. *Lord, may I hear Your voice in the promptings of my conscience.*

HE north wind produces rain, and a backbiting tongue causes angry looks.

—Prov 25:23

OCT. 24

REFLECTION. The north wind in Israel could bring nasty weather, just as a backbiting tongue can produce nasty relationships. We easily use our criticisms and gossip as weapons against each other.

A good rule of thumb is to say ten good and gracious things about another for every criticism that we offer that person.

PRAYER. *Lord, may You bless the person today whom I like least in the world.*

IKE a city that has been breached and made defenseless is the man devoid of self-control. —Prov 25:28

OCT. 25

REFLECTION. There are things that can strongly affect our emotions. We might be angry or hurt or frustrated. These are natural feelings.

What we do with these feelings is what is important. If we let them completely control our reactions, then we are going to get into trouble. We are called to use our emotions to make things better.

PRAYER. *God, may my feelings become a prayer which rises up to You.*

FLATTERING mouth causes devastation. —Prov 26:28b

OCT. 26

REFLECTION. Listening to the flattering words of another can blind us to the realities of our present situation. We have to be honest with ourselves on how things are going.

Furthermore, we have to continuously remind ourselves that we could not possibly do the good that we are doing if it were not for the grace of God.

PRAYER. *May all praise and glory be to You, O Lord.*

S A door turns on its hinges, so does the idler on his bed. —Prov 26:14

OCT. 27

REFLECTION. This proverb presents the image of a lazy person lying on a bed, doing nothing. Our faith should be the source of a profound enthusiasm to change the world in God's image.

This does not mean that we must be working continuously like workaholics. Rather, it is a call to responsibility and commitment.

PRAYER. *May I always do whatever I can to build the Kingdom of God now and in the future.*

N UNRELIABLE messenger engenders trouble, but a trustworthy envoy brings healing. —Prov 13:17

OCT. 28

REFLECTION. Saints Simon and Jude were two of the apostles who carried the message of the coming of the Kingdom to distant lands. They were both martyred for the faith.

With whom have I shared the Good News by word or by deed these days? Am I willing to take the risk of sharing my faith with others?

PRAYER. *Saints Simon and Jude, pray for us.*

EST yourself throughout your life; determine what is bad for you and do not indulge in it. —Sir 37:27

OCT. 29

REFLECTION. It is good to do an examination of conscience each day to determine whether we are really living the values of the Kingdom in our everyday lives.

It is also good to spend a longer period of time (a weekend, a retreat) to take stock of what is positive and what needs improvement in our lives.

PRAYER. *Spirit of God, You see the depths of my heart; lead me in Your ways.*

RATH is cruel and anger is overwhelming, but who can withstand jealousy? —Prov 27:4

OCT. 30

REFLECTION. We should count the blessings we have received each day, possibly even keeping a written record of them. This includes the big blessings as well as the smallest joys that come into our lives.

When we commit ourselves to recognizing how blessed we are, we will not have time to be jealous or envious of others.

PRAYER. *Thank You, Lord, for all the ways that You have blessed me.*

O NOT boast about tomorrow, for you can never be certain what today may bring. —Prov 27:1

OCT. 31

REFLECTION. We would all like to know what the future holds for us and for those whom we love, but we cannot know these things for certain.

Faith is an act of trust in which we profess that no matter what happens, we can be sure that God will never abandon us.

PRAYER. *May I always see Your presence in my life, O Lord, and rejoice in Your love.*

ALL no one happy before his death, for it is by his end that a person becomes known for what he is. —Sir 11:28

NOV. 1

REFLECTION. On this solemnity we celebrate all those who died in the Lord. They might not have been certified as saints by the Church, but they were faithful and true.

It is good every so often to reflect on their good example and to ask them to accompany us in our journey of life.

PRAYER. *All you saints of the Lord, intercede for us.*

ET your generosity also extend to all the living, and do not let your kindness be withheld even from the dead. —Sir 7:33

NOV. 2

REFLECTION. When we pray for our beloved deceased, we join our love to God's love and that love visits the person for whom we are praying.

This loving embrace makes it easier for the person to let go of all the fears and brokenness and to choose eternal love with God in heaven.

PRAYER. *Eternal rest grant unto them, O Lord, and let perpetual light shine upon them.*

O NOT add to the problems of those who are desperate, or keep them waiting for your charity. —Sir 4:3

NOV. 3

REFLECTION. St. Martin de Porres was a wonderful example of charity to the poor. Unlike many of his fellow religious who were highly educated, Martin was able to identify with the lowly and marginalized.

When we offer charity to others, we must be careful not to do it in a way that patronizes those whom we are trying to help.

PRAYER. *May I always affirm the dignity of those to whom I offer assistance.*

THEN you will understand equity and justice as well as righteousness—every good path. —Prov 2:9

NOV. 4

REFLECTION. We are called to be just and righteous in the way we treat others, but we are also called to fight for justice in our society. People are often mistreated because of externals that others use as an excuse to treat them unkindly.

Every person is a brother or sister. Every person was created in the image and likeness of God.

PRAYER. *May I show my respect for everyone whom I meet today.*

STONE is heavy and sand is a dead weight, but heavier than both is a fool's provocation. —Prov 27:3

NOV. 5

REFLECTION. It seems as if some people have a special gift for making our lives difficult. We have to find a strategy of how to deal with them without falling into the trap of being like them.

We must always keep in mind that they are children of God who deserve our respect.

PRAYER. *May I treat the most difficult person in my life with heartfelt dignity.*

HE blows given by a friend are well meant, but the kisses of an enemy are filled with deceit. —Prov 27:6

NOV. 6

REFLECTION. A friend is willing to take a risk and tell me the truth about what is going on, even if that is the last thing I want to hear.

An enemy will treat me nicely and compliment me and pretend to be my best friend, the whole time seeking a way to gain an advantage over me.

PRAYER. *May I be able to read the intentions of other people's hearts.*

HOSE who observe the law are in constant opposition to the wicked man. —Prov 28:4

NOV. 7

REFLECTION. If we hold on to the truth and fight for justice, we will be opposed. It is not that we want to be someone's enemy, but our choices will offend some people.

We have to accept that not everyone will like us. Would that a person who does not like us is acting that way because we are virtuous.

PRAYER. *May I show compassion to all, even to those who consider themselves my enemies.*

FOOL gives free rein to his anger, but a wise man bides his time and calms it.

—Prov 29:11

NOV. 8

REFLECTION. We all become angry at times. Anger is simply an emotion, and it can even be used for the good such as to motivate us to work to make things better.

But if we allow ourselves to be carried away by our anger, then it becomes a destructive force that only creates more division and misunderstandings.

PRAYER. *May I learn to control my anger and not let my anger control me.*

EEP falsehood and lying lips far from me.

—Prov 30:8

NOV. 9

REFLECTION. We don't really like to deal with people for whom honesty is not a great value. We never quite know what to make of what they say to us.

This should motivate us to make our words truthful so that others can know that we are people whom they can trust.

PRAYER. *Purify my lips, O Lord, so that I only speak the truth.*

HE fear of the Lord is glory and exultation, happiness, and a crown of joy.
—Sir 1:11

NOV. 10

REFLECTION. Jesus was obedient to the Father, even to the point of dying on the Cross to show us how much God loves us.

This obedience was not an act of humiliation or servitude, but rather it allowed Jesus to fulfill His destiny to be the most meek and loving person possible.

PRAYER. *Jesus, may I, like You, surrender to the Will of the Father.*

O NOT delay your return to the Lord, and do not put it off from one day to the next.
—Sir 5:7

NOV. 11

REFLECTION. St. Augustine once said, "Lord, grant me chastity, but not yet." We speak about how we should do better in our faith, but these words often turn out to be pious platitudes rather than resolutions.

Today is the day to take stock of our lives. Today is the day to begin to return to the Lord.

PRAYER. *May today be a turning point in my life, O Lord.*

UST as water reflects one's face, so does one human heart reflect another.

—Prov 27:19

NOV. 12

REFLECTION. When we look into a mirror, we see a superficial reflection of who we are. We often see what we want to see.

When we look into the love that those around us have for us, we can discern who we truly are in their hearts and in the heart of God.

PRAYER. *Let me truly see who I am, Lord, in Your love for me.*

F IT is your wish, my child, you can be taught; if you apply yourself, you will become clever.

—Sir 6:32

NOV. 13

REFLECTION. Mother Cabrini dedicated her life to the education and care of the Italian immigrants in this country. She realized that they would be lost without the compassion shown to them by her Sisters.

Sacred Scripture reminds us that every person who is lonely and confused is a brother or sister who needs our love and concern.

PRAYER. *Mother Frances Xavier Cabrini, teach us your ways of compassion.*

IF YOU have understanding, reply to your neighbor, but if not, put your hand over your mouth. —Sir 5:12

NOV. 14

REFLECTION. There is a time to speak and a time to listen. We don't have to say every word that comes to mind, especially when we are a bit confused and emotional.

Holding our tongue and listening and reflecting on what is going on can serve us greatly for it does not make a bad situation worse.

PRAYER. *Guide me Lord, in my speaking and in my silence.*

DO NOT follow your inclinations and energy in pursuing the desires of your heart. —Sir 5:2

NOV. 15

REFLECTION. There are many things we want, or at least we think that we want. Often, they only bring us a sense of disappointment for they are not really what we need.

Just because we desire something does not mean that it is good for us. Sometimes saying "no" to cravings brings us a greater peace and contentment.

PRAYER. *May what I desire be that which I truly need.*

IKE a fluttering sparrow or a swallow in flight, an undeserved curse will never reach home. —Prov 26:2

NOV. 16

REFLECTION. We worry about what others may think of us or say about us. Yet, if their words and judgments are untrue, then they will not stick to us.

Others will think what they want to, and we cannot control that. We must do what is right and refuse to let their unkind comments disturb our peace.

PRAYER. *Lord, may Your's be the only opinion which is important to me.*

O DO what is right and just is more acceptable to the Lord than sacrifice. —Prov 21:3

NOV. 17

REFLECTION. It is very good to pray and to go to Church. But these things are not as important as living our faith in our everyday lives.

Jesus often corrected the Pharisees for performing many religious actions but not converting their hearts and not reaching out to those most in need.

PRAYER. *May my religious actions be consistent with my inner conviction and my outer deeds.*

E CIRCUMSPECT when you visit the house of God. —Eccl 4:17

NOV. 18

REFLECTION. When we go to church, we should bring our joys and sorrows, our good deeds and even our mistakes.

We ask God to bless and magnify the good that we have done, and to forgive and heal whatever bad things we might have done. Then, as we leave church, we ask God for the grace to start over again.

PRAYER. *May our church be a place where I bring who I am and promise to be better.*

HE height of the sky, the breadth of the earth, the depth of the abyss—who can explore them? —Sir 1:3

NOV. 19

REFLECTION. There are wonders far beyond our imagining, and yet God knows all these things. We should be filled with a sense of awe and wonder.

Possibly the most incredible thing in all of this is that God Who is so great and wonderful would care about each of us as a parent cares for a child.

PRAYER. *How great Thou art, O Lord, how great Thou art!*

O NOT be the cause of harm in either great or small matters. —Sir 5:15

NOV. 20

REFLECTION. It is easy to convince ourselves that we can do something because it is not really all that bad. This type of logic is poisonous for one bad thing leads to another thing, often worse.

If we want to change our ways, we must commit ourselves not to do anything bad, be it great or small.

PRAYER. *May all of my actions be filled with Your grace, O Lord.*

AKE care not to be led astray and humiliated as a result of your own stupidity. —Sir 13:8

NOV. 21

REFLECTION. We have to live with our choices, for good or bad. This is why we should be careful when we are making important decisions.

We should pray and ponder, ask advice, and weigh probabilities. After we have done all that, we should place it all in the hands of God.

PRAYER. *Guide me along the right path, O Lord, and lead me with Your constant guidance.*

O NOT envy the success of a sinner, for you can never be sure what his end will be. —Sir 9:11

NOV. 22

REFLECTION. Those who choose the wrong path often do better in this world than those who try to live a good life. It does not seem fair.

Yet, there will be a reckoning at the end of time. At the last judgment, we will have to live forever with the consequences of our choices.

PRAYER. *Let me not envy the proud or arrogant, but rather let me choose a life of virtue.*

LMSGIVING is like a signet ring to him (God), and he cherishes kindness like the apple of his eye. —Sir 17:22

NOV. 23

REFLECTION. At the end of November, as we celebrate Thanksgiving, it is a good time to remember that our gratitude to God should be expressed through our outreach to those in need.

Tertullian, an early Christian author, reminds us that what is in excess is robbed from the poor. We have received blessings from God to share blessings with others.

PRAYER. *Thank You, Lord, for the opportunity to serve You in the person of the poor.*

RAISE is uttered only by the tongues of the wise; and the Lord himself prompts it.

—Sir 15:10

NOV. 24

REFLECTION. We sometimes act as if praising another would somehow subtract from our self-worth.

Praising another is one of the most generous and honest things that we can do, for we do not receive anything in return. Yet, it builds up the spirit of the one who is praised which is a godly thing.

PRAYER. *May I celebrate and acclaim all the good that is around me.*

HEN there is no wood, the fire goes out, and when there is no talebearer, quarreling ceases.

—Prov 26:20

NOV. 25

REFLECTION. It is easy to look upon the person who always gossips and to condemn that person.

But what about ourselves? Do we sometimes spread the wrong things? Do we secretly enjoy a piece of juicy gossip? It is easy to participate in gossip to a lesser degree and to absolve ourselves of any culpability.

PRAYER. *May I not say even the smallest thing that would hurt another person's reputation.*

ANY are the plans in a human mind, but it is the purpose of the Lord that will prevail. —Prov 19:21

NOV. 26

REFLECTION. It is not that God has everything planned in our lives as if we were robots.

Rather, God has a plan for us and we are also given free will, and those two work together. God is also the ultimate opportunist, for God can use even our mistakes to bring us to a greater fidelity.

PRAYER. *Guide me, O Lord, in Your ways, teach me Your paths.*

IKE one who lifts up a stray dog by the ears is he who meddles in another person's quarrel. —Prov 26:17

NOV. 27

REFLECTION. When you lift up a stray dog, you never know how it will respond. It might very well attack you.

Likewise, when you get involved in someone else's quarrel, you could easily end up regretting it. You will have made yourself the enemy of at least one person, if not both.

PRAYER. *Lord, let me be prudent in taking sides when there is a difficulty.*

E WHOSE guide is wisdom will come through safely. —Prov 28:26

NOV. 28

REFLECTION. Life is not always easy to navigate. We can become confused by the changing world that surrounds us, and we can be tempted to buy into its values.

If we hold on to the Lord's Wisdom, then we will know for sure that we are headed in the right direction.

PRAYER. *Guide me, Wisdom of God, along the path of my life.*

NE who remains stubborn despite frequent reproof will suddenly be crushed beyond hope of repair. —Prov 29:1

NOV. 29

REFLECTION. As much as God is patient, there does come a time when we will face the consequences of the choices that we have made.

It is not that God rejoices in our tragic fate, but God has given us free will. For God it is a tragedy every time one of His beloved children makes the wrong choices.

PRAYER. *Open my ears and my heart so that I might hear Your call to repentance.*

HEN an intelligent man hears words of wisdom, he praises them and adds to them. —Sir 21:15

NOV. 30

REFLECTION. The apostle St. Andrew heard what Jesus taught and saw the wonders He did, and he called his brother St. Peter to follow Jesus.

Who have I called to follow Jesus in these days? With whom have I shared the Good News that we are forgiven and loved and called to God's glory?

PRAYER. *Lord, may I have the courage to proclaim Your Good News to those around me.*

O NOT seek to learn what is too sublime for you; investigate not those things that are beyond your scope. —Sir 3:21

DEC. 1

REFLECTION. There are limits to what we can understand. We should be curious and seek to know more, but we must also be humble and recognize that there are things beyond our ability.

This is not a surrender to ignorance nor a question of giving up. Rather, it is an acknowledgment that we are creatures and not the Creator.

PRAYER. *Let me know what I can know, Lord, and accept what is beyond me.*

O NOT grieve one who is hungry or exasperate someone in distress. —Sir 4:2

DEC. 2

REFLECTION. Hurting people who are already in pain is not simply a question of mocking them. It could also be that we simply ignore them, treating them as if they don't exist.

Our goal in a world in which so many people are hurting is to heal it, one heart at a time.

PRAYER. *Send me forth, O Lord, to make this world a better place.*

HE fruit of the righteous is a tree of life, and the wise person wins souls.

—Prov 11:30

DEC. 3

REFLECTION. The most important way to evangelize, to proclaim the Good News, is to live a good and wise life.

Words are cheap, and sometimes those who proclaim the Gospel do so in a way that actually repels people. If we live a good, quiet, virtuous life, people will see what we are doing and want to do it as well.

PRAYER. *May I always live that which I say that I am, Lord.*

EVER attempt to speak what is contrary to the truth, but rather feel ashamed at your own ignorance. —Sir 4:25

DEC. 4

REFLECTION. We do not know everything, and one of the most impressive things is to hear someone admit this.

If we want to live in the truth, we must continue to study and reflect upon what our faith teaches. We must examine how others are living it and commit ourselves to changing our own ways to reflect it better.

PRAYER. *Guide me, Lord, so that I might live in Your truth.*

HE Lord disciplines those whom he loves, just as a father chastises a beloved son. —Prov 3:12

DEC. 5

REFLECTION. The most painful thing God could ever do to us is to let us feel the consequences of our own sins: loneliness and selfishness.

It is not that God wants us to suffer, but God does want us to realize what a mess we are making of our lives. God is, in a sense, casting us a lifeline when God disciplines us.

PRAYER. *Correct me, Lord, of those things which drag me away from Your life and love.*

GENEROUS person will be enriched; he who refreshes others will also be refreshed. —Prov 11:25

DEC. 6

REFLECTION. On this feast of St. Nicholas, we remember how he was generous with those who were in need when he was a bishop in Asia Minor. This is why he became the model for Santa Claus.

A possible goal today would be to seek out someone who is in any form of need and try to respond to that person's poverty.

PRAYER. *St. Nicholas, pray for us.*

ISDOM is a tree of life to all who embrace her, and blessed are all who hold her fast. —Prov 3:18

DEC. 7

REFLECTION. St. Ambrose was a famous wisdom figure in the early Church. His preaching, in fact, inspired St. Augustine to convert to the faith.

It would be good to read a biography of these and other saints every so often so that we might learn about their wisdom and follow their example.

PRAYER. *St. Ambrose, guide us in our search for wisdom.*

THE Lord loves the pure of heart.

—Prov 22:11

DEC. 8

REFLECTION. The Blessed Virgin Mary was protected from the damage of sin from the moment of her conception. That is why she was able to respond to God's call through Gabriel with such generosity.

We can ask her help to purify our hearts so that our response to God's call might be ever more generous.

PRAYER. *Mary, the Immaculate Conception, intercede for us.*

IT IS better to be short of sense and God-fearing than to be highly intelligent and violate the law.

—Sir 19:24

DEC. 9

REFLECTION. St. Juan Diego was a simple Native American man, yet it was to him that the Blessed Virgin Mary appeared at Guadalupe. She entrusted her image to him to share with the world.

It is not just the educated or privileged who can change the world. Often it is the simple ones who transform how we see things.

PRAYER. *St. Juan Diego, pray for us.*

HE fear of the Lord is the full measure of wisdom; she intoxicates people with her fruits. —Sir 1:16

DEC. 10

REFLECTION. We always have to remember that the fear of God is not to be afraid of God, but rather it is to recognize God's greatness.

When we are filled with awe at Who God is and what God has done, it is almost as if we are drunk with God's glory.

PRAYER. *Batter my heart, three-personed God.*

HE sands of the sea, the drops of rain, and the days of eternity—who can count them? —Sir 1:2

DEC. 11

REFLECTION. Astronomers tell us that there are millions of galaxies, each of which could contain millions of stars. This is all mind-boggling.

Yet, the myriads of stars are as nothing in light of all of the other wonders that God has created, and even all of that is as nothing compared to the glory of God.

PRAYER. *May I ponder the wonders of creation and even more its Creator.*

KINDLY glance gives joy to the heart, and good news refreshes the bones. —Prov 15:30

DEC. 12

REFLECTION. Our Lady appeared to St. Juan Diego at Guadalupe to send encouragement and consolation to a population that had been sorely treated by the invasion and conquest of Mexico.

It is a true consolation to have a heavenly mother who fully understands the needs of our hearts and who responds to us with an unconditional, overflowing love.

PRAYER. *Our Lady of Guadalupe, teach us your ways of gentleness and compassion.*

EVER do anything without careful deliberation, but once you have acted, do not regret your decision. —Sir 32:19

DEC. 13

REFLECTION. There is a tendency to second guess ourselves after we have made a decision. We wonder if we thought through all the possible consequences.

We can console ourselves with the fact that even if we have made the wrong choice, God can still use it. God even uses sinful choices as an opportunity to show us greater mercy.

PRAYER. *Lord, quiet my doubts and teach me to trust in You.*

THE love of the Lord is glorious Wisdom, he apportions her to those to whom he appears, that they may see him.

—Sir 1:10

DEC. 14

REFLECTION. The Spanish mystics Saints John of the Cross and Teresa of Avila spoke of the profound love which God has for us.

St. John taught that the ascent into the love of God is found through a life of virtue, living in faith, hope and charity. It is that which most pleases the Lord.

PRAYER. *Through the intercession of St. John of the Cross, may I learn true humility of heart.*

THE wealthy, the noble, and the poor achieve their glory in the fear of the Lord.

—Sir 10:22

DEC. 15

REFLECTION. We are all the same when it comes to serving the Lord. No matter how rich, intelligent, or strong one is, we are called to recognize the Lord as our God and our all.

Special abilities and circumstances can even be a hindrance because we can begin to think that we can do it on our own without God's help.

PRAYER. *Lord, all I have is from You, and all I possess I return to You.*

RUST him, and he will help you; follow a straight path and hope in him. —Sir 2:6

DEC. 16

REFLECTION. The wisdom figures of the Old Testament warned of the danger of wandering to the left or right when we should follow the true path to the Lord.

This often happens when we feel sorry for ourselves or bored or just curious about what another path might hold. We must affirm our hope and trust in the Lord.

PRAYER. *Lead me home, O Lord, to the joys of Your Kingdom.*

ATRED stirs up strife, but love overlooks all offenses. —Prov 10:12

DEC. 17

REFLECTION. How do we destroy the power of hatred and evil in the world? Evil is not something that exists; it is an absence (of good and love).

How do we destroy an absence? We add those things which are lacking, in this case good and love. This is the lesson of the cross.

PRAYER. *Let my love, O Lord, conquer whatever hatred or evil might reside in my heart.*

ERFUME and incense gladden the heart, and friendship's sweetness comforts the soul. —Prov 27:9

DEC. 18

REFLECTION. A good friend is someone who laughs when we laugh, cries when we cry, but most of all gives us a good example of living a life of integrity and compassion.

When we experience that, it is easier to choose the ways of the Lord for we know that we are not alone in this journey.

PRAYER. *May I experience Your consolation, O Lord, through the love of my friends.*

NLY one is wise and greatly to be feared, seated upon his throne—the Lord. —Sir 1:8

DEC. 19

REFLECTION. We are faced with difficulties and fears and doubts every day of our lives. Yet, when we keep the providence of God in mind, these fade into their true perspective.

In spite of all the confusion in our lives, we have to trust that God is in charge and God will bring things to a loving conclusion.

PRAYER. *Lord, help me to trust when things are not going well.*

DD nothing to God's words, lest he reprove you and expose you as a fraud. —Prov 30:6

DEC. 20

REFLECTION. It is easy to read into Sacred Scripture and see what we would like to see. Doing that means that we are proclaiming ourselves and not the Lord.

We have to have the humility to let God speak to us, even if what we are hearing is uncomfortable and challenges us to change our ways.

PRAYER. *Speak to me, O Lord, and let me hear Your message.*

S SILVER is tested by a crucible and gold by a furnace, so too is a man tested by the praise he is given.—Prov 27:21

DEC. 21

REFLECTION. You would think that praise is something that would be good for a person to receive, but it is a double-edged sword. While it builds up one's spirit, it can also turn one's head.

All good comes from God. Our talents and the opportunity for us to do good are God's gift to us, not our own possession.

PRAYER. *All praise to You, Lord, for all that You have done through me.*

HE wonders of the Lord can be neither diminished nor increased, nor are they possible to fathom. —Sir 18:6

DEC. 22

REFLECTION. As we approach the celebration of Christmas, we can reflect on the idea that God, Who is beyond anything we could ever understand, decided to join us in this world and become a little child.

It makes no sense that God, the all-powerful, would become a helpless child, and yet that is the message of Christmas.

PRAYER. *May this Christmas fill me with a child-like sense of awe and wonder.*

OR the Lord is compassionate and merciful; he forgives sins and saves in the time of distress. —Sir 2:11

DEC. 23

REFLECTION. Jesus told Nicodemus that God had sent His Son into the world not to condemn it, but to bring it to life eternal.

This explains why Jesus was born in Bethlehem: so that we might be saved by His love which He showed to us in His birth as well as in His death on the Cross.

PRAYER. *Shower Your healing love upon me, O Lord, so that I might have life eternal.*

MY CHILD, in the practice of humility do not neglect your self-respect, value yourself at your true worth.

—Sir 10:28

DEC. 24

REFLECTION. Humility does not mean self-degradation. We should not put ourselves down thinking that this is what God wants of us.

God created us to live in His dignity, and He thought enough of us to send His Son to die for us on the Cross. We are all precious in God's eyes.

PRAYER. *Thank You, Lord, for the incredible dignity You have given me.*

THE Lord created me as the firstborn of his ways, before the oldest of his works.

—Prov 8:22

DEC. 25

REFLECTION. When the writers of the early Church tried to explain how Jesus could have been God before He was conceived in the womb of the Blessed Virgin Mary, they taught that everything that the Old Testament authors said about wisdom, they were really saying about Jesus.

Jesus is the eternal wisdom in the flesh.

PRAYER. *Jesus, eternal wisdom and child born of Mary, have mercy on us.*

MAN of knowledge prevails over one who has strength. —Prov 24:5b

DEC. 26

REFLECTION. St. Stephen was the first martyr of the Church, and he died giving witness to the truth when he preached in Jerusalem.

As he was dying, he forgave his persecutors and placed his life in God's hands, just as Jesus did. This reminds us that when the faithful suffer, Jesus is suffering with them.

PRAYER. *St. Stephen, first martyr of the Church, pray for us.*

UARD your heart with all possible vigilance, for from it flow the wellsprings of life. —Prov 4:23

DEC. 27

REFLECTION. While we could describe the relationship of most of the apostles and Jesus as one of faith and obedience, we can only speak of love when we speak of John.

In the Letters of John, we hear that God is love, and that God taught us what love really is when God gave His only Son to die for our sins.

PRAYER. *Take me to Yourself, Lord, imprison me, for I, except You enthrall me, shall never be free.*

MONG the winged creatures the bee is small, but its produce is the choicest of sweet harvests. —Sir 11:3

DEC. 28

REFLECTION. Little bees are so small and insignificant, but they produce a precious gift of honey and wax in abundance.

The children of Bethlehem, the holy innocents, were also small and insignificant, but by their silent witness against the hatred and pain that caused their deaths, they proclaimed a new era of justice and peace.

PRAYER. *I pray for all the innocents of the world who suffer from injustice.*

IGHT to the death for truth, and the Lord God will ally himself on your side. —Sir 4:28

DEC. 29

REFLECTION. St. Thomas á Becket died insisting upon fidelity to the Church's teachings, even when this put his life in great danger.

We could say that St. Thomas lost, for he was killed. The more profound truth is that he won, for he never abandoned the truth as he knew it.

PRAYER. *St. Thomas á Becket, pray for us.*

HE rich man may believe he is wise, but the poor man with discernment will see through him. —Prov 28:11

DEC. 30

REFLECTION. It is often the simple people who are able to see past pretentions and discern the real matter at hand. This might be why the Blessed Virgin often appeared to the simple: they were ready to listen to her message.

We are called to simplify our lives and to allow our faith to be childlike.

PRAYER. *May I always approach You, O Lord, with humility and simplicity.*

HE fear of the Lord gladdens the heart, bestowing happiness and joy and a long life. —Sir 1:12

DEC. 31

REFLECTION. As we wish people a Happy New Year, we often speak of happiness and prosperity and good health and a long life.

Yet, all of these blessings would be meaningless if they were not lived in and through Jesus. He is the purpose of our life and its ultimate goal.

PRAYER. *Jesus, You are the Alpha and the Omega of my life.*

HOLY WEEK

PALM SUNDAY

ISDOM enables the poor man to hold his head high and to take his seat among the great. —Sir 11:1

REFLECTION. The crowd proclaimed Jesus as the Son of David, the Messiah, when He entered Jerusalem. Yet, He came in riding on a young donkey, a sign of His humility.

When we do the Lord's Will, we must remember to be humble and to keep in mind that we can only do it if we are guided by His Wisdom.

PRAYER. *Jesus, Son of David, please teach me Your true humility.*

HOLY THURSDAY

"

OME and partake of my food and taste the wine that I have prepared!" —Prov 9:5

REFLECTION. Just as Lady Wisdom prepared a meal for the simple so that they might be one with her, so Jesus invites His disciples to eat of the bread which had become His Body and drink of the wine which had become His Blood.

Jesus offers His disciples His wisdom, but even more. He offers them His very self.

PRAYER. *O Holy Banquet, in which Christ is received, the memory of His passion is recalled.*

GOOD FRIDAY

OW great is the mercy of the Lord and the forgiveness he offers to those who return to him!

—Sir 17:29

REFLECTION. In the Gospel of John, the reason why Jesus dies on the Cross is that we would never believe that we were forgiven and loved by God if Jesus had not died out of love for us.

This means that the Cross is the clearest sign of how much God loves us: He loves us to death.

PRAYER. *May I live in the love of He Who died out of love for me.*

HOLY SATURDAY

HO can truly say, "I have cleansed my heart, and I am purified of all sin?" **—Prov 20:9**

REFLECTION. On this quiet and somewhat lonesome day, we realize that something is missing, almost as if a loved one had died in our family.

It is good to use this empty time to reflect on why Jesus died for us and how we must respond to that act of love.

PRAYER. *Lord Jesus, may I die to myself so that I might rise with You.*

EASTER SUNDAY

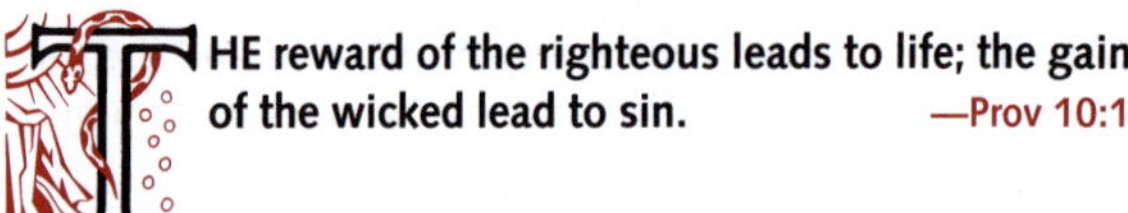

THE reward of the righteous leads to life; the gains of the wicked lead to sin. —Prov 10:16

REFLECTION. Jesus, the righteous One, has triumphed over death. Sin and death have been swallowed up by the love and life of our Saving Lord.

Jesus is risen, Alleluia, Alleluia. We have no need to run to the empty tomb for we know in our minds and hearts that Jesus is truly risen.

PRAYER. *My heart cries out Alleluia, Alleluia, Alleluia!*